1

GW00806324

Sprachbrücke

Deutsch als Fremdsprache

Wortschatz kontrastiv
Deutsch — Englisch

bearbeitet von Eva-Maria Jenkins
übersetzt von Veronica Kerr

Klett Edition Deutsch

Sprachbrücke 1 Lehrwerk für Deutsch als Fremdsprache

von
Gudula Mebus, Andreas Pauldrach, Marlene Rall, Dietmar Rösler
in Zusammenarbeit mit
Heinke Behal-Thomsen, Jürgen Genuneit

Wortschatz kontrastiv: Deutsch – Englisch
von
Eva-Maria Jenkins, Veronica Kerr

English abbreviations:

etc.	etcetera
ie.	that is
eg.	for example
Amer.	American
pl.	plural

German abbreviations:

AS	Auftaktseite (introductory page)
f	femininum (feminine)
m	maskulinum (masculine)
Sg.	Singular (singular)
Pl.	Plural (plural)
Akk.	Akkusativ (accusative)
Dat.	Dativ (dative)
Gen.	Genitiv (genitive)
i. d. Bed.	in dieser Bedeutung (in this meaning)
nur 3. Person	nur dritte Person (only 3rd person)

Signs:

=	equals
≠	the opposite
*	irregular verb

1. Auflage 1   4   3   2   1 | 1992   91   90   89

Alle Drucke dieser Auflage können nebeneinander benutzt werden, sie sind untereinander unverändert. Die letzte Zahl bezeichnet das Jahr des Druckes.
© Verlag Klett Edition Deutsch GmbH, München 1989. Alle Rechte vorbehalten.
Druck: Gutmann + Co., Heilbronn. Printed in Germany.
ISBN 3-12-557510-9

Information for the user

What is in the Vocabulary Resource Book of "Sprachbrücke 1"?

1. Words and Phrases

All the words and phrases in the texts and exercises of the lessons as well as the grammatical terminology are to be found in the Resource Book with the corresponding translation.

As a rule each word/phrase is put in once only, that is, at its first occurrence (reading from top to bottom and from left to right). After that it is assumed that the word/phrase is known. To make it easier to find, the individual steps in the lessons are indicated: AS = Auftaktseite (the introductory page), A1, A2, B1 etc.

Words which occur in the introductory pages and appear again later in a part of the lesson are put in twice; the introductory page to each lesson summarizes its theme, and is often only used for revision purposes.

Unfamiliar vocabulary items in the texts which are to be used explicitly for reading or listening comprehension (marked 🔟 or 🦜 in the book) are not put in; the purpose of this type of text-study is to learn how to deal with unfamiliar words or phrases in texts. These can often be elicited from the context or simply skinned over.

We have given a complete translation of some illustrative poems with particularly difficult vocabulary so that you do not have to work laboriously through individual parts, but can understand them in their entirety.

The names which have been made up in the context of the fictitious country "Lilaland" are compiled in a list on page 10.

The new word/phrase appears first with the meaning of its use in the lesson (the context example) with idiomatic (not word-for-word) translation, and only after that as an individual word.

Nouns are given with their articles and plural forms (from Lesson 1 onwards in the normal short form as in a dictionary). Do not be confused by these forms, but up to Lesson 4 simply read them without paying too much attention to them. Plural forms are then introduced in Lesson 4 of the text book.

Irregular verbs are indicated with the sign *. You will find a list of irregular verbs on page 226 of the text book. Irregular and separable verbs are given in the conjugation of the first and third persons; incomplete conjugation paradigms will be pointed out.

With professions the feminine form is given in brackets. For example: der Lehrer, – (in f) – teacher.

You will come across a peculiarity of the German language in the first lesson in the text book: the possibility of joining two words together (noun + noun, noun + adjective etc.) to form a new compound word. These words are called "zusammengesetzte Wörter" (that is literally, "words put together"). In the beginning it is not always easy to recognize the structure and the meaning of these "words put together". A way of helping you to practise analysing these compound words is used in the Vocabulary Resource Book: a little hook to the right (for example: das Wörter‿buch – the dictionary) marks the join between the two nouns forming the word. Then when you know that the second element (the one on the right) in the compound word states the basic meaning (the "Wörter<u>buch</u>" is a "<u>Buch</u>", a book) you recognize the basic meaning of the word even if you do not know the first element. As the possibilities for compounds are almost unlimited in German, and many of these words are made up on the spur of the moment and are unlikely to be found in a dictionary (eg. see the commentary on the concept of "Begrüßungstheater" – Theatre of Welcome – on page 64), it helps if one can at least look up the base-word in a dictionary.

It is somewhat similar with the verbs: the joining place of the so-called "separable verbs" is marked with a little hook to the left (eg. mit‿bringen – to bring or take with you, etc.). Thus one can recognize the base-verb. But be careful! These little hooks are only a graphic aid: they are not part of the script of written German.

2. Certificate Vocabulary

If you want to pass the examination for the "Zertifikat Deutsch als Fremdsprache" (Certificate of German as a Foreign Language), then you must pay attention to the words printed in heavy type in the Vocabulary Resource Book; they are the ones assumed to be known for the Certificate. You can ask your teacher which of the other words you should be able to use competently, and which ones it is enough just to understand.

3. The Boxes

In the boxes particular aspects of the vocabulary, ie. word-building, meaning, use, are pointed out as an extension to the textbook and the workbook:

In the contrastive-comparative boxes meaning and use of the German words are contrasted with those of the mother tongue. For example: German: **Zahl** or **Nummer** – English: number (page 22).

In the boxes on meaning you find explanations of the particular culture-specific "German" meaning of a concept. For example: **Federbett** – feather bed (page 111).

In the boxes on structure you find short summaries of the word-building rules. For example: **Städte und ihre Einwohner** – Towns and their inhabitants (page 49).

In revision boxes homonyms, that is, words with the same sound but different meanings, and similar sounding phrases from earlier lessons are contrasted with each other. For example: **gerade** – just; straight (page 144), **jemanden um einen Gefallen bitten** – to ask a favour of someone, **jemandem einen Gefallen tun** – to do someone a favour (page 131).

How can I work with the Vocabulary Resource Book?

1. The Resource Book as a help to learning and understanding

The vocabulary given is considered to be a help in understanding and learning for the homework done out of class. Only use the Resource Book in the lesson if your teacher asks you to. Otherwise always try first to understand new words and phrases from the context and with the help of the explanations in the class lesson. Take the opportunity to practise (listening) comprehension in this way and to ask questions in German if there is something you have not understood. You learn the language exponents necessary to do this in the first lessons of "Sprachbrücke".

From the beginning you should always learn the nouns with their articles and later (from Lesson 4) also with their plural forms.

Learn the irregular verbs at first with their 1st and 3rd persons, given in brackets. After a time, when the regularity of the forms of conjugation is familiar to you, you only need to learn the simple past and the past participle. (List of irregular verbs: Textbook, page 226 ff.).

Do not learn the words in isolation. Memorize them through the examples of their use in the textbook. In this way you will automatically adapt the correct use of the words and be able to transfer them more easily to other contexts.

2. The Vocabulary Resource Book used thematically

The Vocabulary Resource Book is more than just a list of words. As the Lessons and the constituent parts of "Sprachbrücke" are arranged according to specific themes, the words are automatically in a thematic order. Be conscious of this when you are learning vocabulary; words placed in a thematic context can be remembered more easily . With a lesson or part of a lesson to hand you can put together word fields for yourself as an aid to learning, and these you can extend again and again.

For example: the theme "Essen" (meals, food) in Lesson 9. A work-sheet to help learn this vocabulary could look something like this:

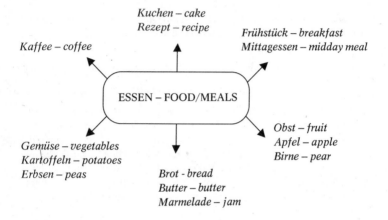

Kuchen – cake
Rezept – recipe

Frühstück – breakfast
Mittagessen – midday meal

Kaffee – coffee

ESSEN – FOOD/MEALS

Obst – fruit
Apfel – apple
Birne – pear

Gemüse – vegetables
Kartoffeln – potatoes
Erbsen – peas

Brot - bread
Butter – butter
Marmelade – jam

The aim is not to draw up complete lists, but to use the conscious perception of thematic contexts as an aid to learning and memorizing. The alphabetical word list can also be used to extend the thematic lists: After the word "Arbeit" (work), for example, you find many compound words (with "Arbeit") from different lessons.

So, now we wish much enjoyment and every success in learning German.

Informationen für Lehrerinnen und Lehrer

Was finden die Deutschlernenden in diesem Buch?

1. Wörter und Wendungen

Sie finden alle Wörter und Wendungen aus den Lektionstexten und Übungen von „Sprachbrücke" Band 1 sowie die im Buch benutzte Grammatikterminologie mit englischer Übersetzung.

In der Regel wurde jedes Wort/jede Wendung einmal aufgenommen, und zwar jeweils beim erstmaligen Vorkommen (gelesen von oben nach unten und von links nach rechts). In der Folge wird das Wort/die Wendung als bekannt vorausgesetzt. Um das Auffinden zu erleichtern, wird im Wortschatz auf die einzelnen Lektionsschritte (AS = Auftaktseite, A1, A2, B1 . . .) verwiesen.

Wörter, die sowohl auf der Auftaktseite der Lektionen als auch später im Lektionsteil vorkommen, wurden doppelt aufgenommen: die Auftaktseite, die das Thema einer Lektion zusammenfaßt, wird im Unterricht oft erst zur Wiederholung eingesetzt.

Nicht aufgenommen wurden unbekannte Vokabeln aus Texten, mit denen ausdrücklich das Leseverstehen bzw. das Hörverstehen (im Buch gekennzeichnet mit 📖 bzw. mit 🎧) geübt werden soll, denn Ziel dieser Art von Textarbeit ist es, daß die Kursteilnehmer/innen lernen, unbekannte Textelemente aus Bekanntem zu entschlüsseln oder einfach darüber hinwegzulesen bzw. hinwegzuhören.

Einige illustrative Gedichte mit besonders schwierigem Wortschatz wurden übersetzt, um den Lernenden das Verständnis zu erleichtern.

Die Kunstnamen im Zusammenhang mit dem fiktiven Land „Lilaland" wurden auf Seite 10 in einer Übersicht zusammengestellt.

Das neue Wort/Die neue Wendung erscheint zunächst im Verwendungszusammenhang (Kontextbeispiel) der Lektion mit idiomatischer (also nicht wort-wörtlicher) Übersetzung, danach erst als Einzelstichwort.

Substantive werden mit Artikel und Pluralangabe (schon ab Lektion 1 in der in Wörterbüchern üblichen Kurzform) angegeben. Für wiederholendes Wortschatzlernen erschien uns dieses Vorgehen nützlich. Weisen Sie die Kursteilnehmer/innen jedoch darauf hin, daß sie diese Formen zunächst ignorieren dürfen. In Lektion 4 des Lehrbuchs werden die Pluralformen eingeführt und erklärt.

Bei Berufsbezeichnungen wird die feminine Form in Klammern angegeben, z. B.: der Techniker, – (in f).

Unregelmäßige Verben sind mit dem Zeichen * gekennzeichnet. Die Liste der unregelmäßigen Verben befindet sich im Lehrbuch, Seite 226 ff. Unregelmäßige und trennbare Verben werden mit den Konjugationsformen der ersten und dritten Person angegeben; auf unvollständige Konjugationsparadigmen wird hingewiesen.

Um den Lernenden zu helfen, zusammengesetzte Wörter und ihre Bedeutung zu erkennen oder nachzuschlagen, wurde ein grafisches Hilfsmittel benutzt: Ein Häkchen nach rechts (Wörter‿buch) markiert bei Substantiven die Fuge zwischen den beiden Wörtern. Das Grundwort wird auf diese Weise sofort erkennbar.

Etwas Ähnliches gilt für die Verben: Bei den trennbaren Verben ist die Fugenstelle mit einem Häkchen nach links (mit‿bringen) markiert.

Vielleicht müssen Sie die Lernenden wiederholt darauf hinweisen, daß es sich bei diesem Zeichen nicht um ein Schriftzeichen der deutschen Sprache handelt, sondern nur um ein grafisches Hilfsmittel zur Analyse von Wörtern (siehe dazu auch „Information for the user", Seite 3).

2. Zertifikatswortschatz

Der Wortschatz aus der Wortliste des ‚Zertifikats Deutsch als Fremdsprache' ist fett gedruckt. Bei allen anderen Wörtern sind Hinweise für die Lernenden, welche Wörter sie aktiv beherrschen sollen und bei welchen es genügt, sie nur zu verstehen, sicher nützlich.

3. Kästchen

In den Kästchen wird ergänzend zu Lehrbuch und Arbeitsbuch auf besondere Aspekte des Wortschatzes, d. h. Wortbildung, Orthographie, Bedeutung und Gebrauch hingewiesen:

In den kontrastiv-vergleichenden Kästchen werden Bedeutung und Gebrauch des deutschen Wortes dem englischen Wort gegenübergestellt. Zum Beispiel: Deutsch: **Zahl** oder **Nummer** – Englisch: number (Seite 22).

Die Bedeutungskästchen enthalten Erklärungen zur besonderen kulturspezifischen „deutschen" Bedeutung eines Begriffs. Zum Beispiel: **Federbett** (Seite 111).

Strukturkästchen bringen kleine Übersichten zu Wortbildungsregularitäten. Zum Beispiel: **Städte und ihre Einwohner** (Seite 49).

In Wiederholungskästchen werden Homonyme, das heißt gleichlautende Wörter mit verschiedener Bedeutung und ähnlich lautende Wendungen aus früheren Lektionen wieder aufgenommen und einander gegenübergestellt. Zum Beispiel: **gerade** (Seite 144) oder **jemandem einen Gefallen tun – jemanden um einen Gefallen bitten –** (Seite 131).

Wie kann man mit dem Wortschatz arbeiten?

1. Der Wortschatz als Lern- und Verständnishilfe

Der kontrastive Wortschatz ist als Verständnishilfe und als Lernhilfe beim häuslichen Nacharbeiten gedacht. Die Lernenden sollten ihn nur in den Unterricht mitbringen, wenn Sie es ausdrücklich wünschen. Ermutigen Sie Ihre Kursteilnehmer/innen, Bedeutungen immer wieder im Unterricht auf deutsch zu erfragen: Die Redemittel dazu lernen sie schon in den ersten Lektionen von „Sprachbrücke 1".

Weitere Hinweise für die Lernenden enthält die „Information for the user".

2. Thematische Wortschatzarbeit

Da die Lektionen und Bausteine von Sprachbrücke jeweils bestimmten Themen zugeordnet sind, ergibt die Zusammenstellung der Wörter eine thematische Ordnung.

Beim Wortschatzlernen sollten die Lernenden bewußt auf diesen Aspekt achten: Thematisch zusammenhängende Wörter kann man sich besser merken.

Fordern Sie die Lernenden auf, anhand einer Lektion oder einiger Bausteine Wortfelder zusammenzustellen, die nach und nach ergänzt werden können. Ein Beispiel zum Thema „Essen" finden Sie am Schluß der „Information for the user".

Auch die alphabetische Wortliste kann ergänzend hinzugezogen werden. Dort findet man häufig ganze Wortfamilien, zum Beispiel: Arbeit, arbeiten, Arbeiter, Arbeitsbuch, Arbeitsleistung, Arbeitsplatz usw.

Kunstnamen	Fictitious names
Lilaland	*Fictitious country. The Klingers, a German family, take a trip there.*
Lilaländer	*inhabitant of* Lilaland
lilaländisch	*adjective of* Lilaland
Lilastadt	*town in* Lilaland
Sprachinstitut „Lila"	*Language institute in* Lilastadt *where one can learn German.*
Lila Welle	*Parallel organization to* Deutsche Welle, *the German external radio service.*
Alli Alga Bina Boto Dr. Dadu Koto Kana Frau Larsen Lara Lenzi Frau Mito Nuri Nabu Tomi Tossu Herr Zara	*inhabitants of* Lilaland
Emma Regula	*Lady who specializes in grammar rules and tables.*

Other invented names are Bel *(Lesson 1, F1) and* Owi *(Lesson 4, C9).*

A German family visits Lilaland:
Hans Klinger, *Businessman: Marketer of Tourism.*
His wife: Gerda Klinger, *Journalist.*
Their two children: Beate Klinger *(16 years)* and Peter *(12 years).*

AS Großes Vornamen Buch

> Book of First Names
> Großes (= large) *might be 'The Complete Book of . . .' in English.*

Andrea — *first name for a female*
Zacharias — *first name for a male*
Namen von A–Z — Names from A to Z
Von Abel bis Zwicknagel — From Abel to Zwicknagel
Lexikon deutscher Familiennamen — Dictionary of German Surnames
Das Berufe-Alphabet — Alphabetical list of occupations
der Astronaut, -en — astronaut
der Bademeister, - — baths attendant
der Clown, -s — clown

A 1 **Guten Morgen!** — Good morning!
der Morgen — morning
Guten Tag! — Hello!

> *The Germans use „Hallo!" but only to close friends.*

der Tag, -e — day
Guten Abend! — Good evening!
der Abend, -e — evening
A 2 die Anmeldung, -en — registration
das Sprachinstitut, -e — the language institute
die Sprache, -n — language
Anmeldung im Sprachinstitut — registering at the language institute
lila — lilac, purple
Hören Sie bitte! — Please listen.

> *Note: The polite form **Sie** has an initial capital.*

hören — to listen; hear
bitte — please
Wie ist Ihr Name? — What is your name?
Mein Name ist . . . — My name is . . .
mein, meine — my
der Name, -n — name
Wie heißen Sie? — What are you called?
Ich heiße . . . — I am called . . .
heißen — to be called
Wie bitte? — Pardon?
Ist das Ihr Familienname? — Is that your surname?

1

der Familien‚name, -n	surname
Ja.	Yes.
Und wie ist Ihr Vorname?	And what is your first name?
der Vor‚name, -n	Christian name, first name
und	and
danke	thank you
der Kurs, -e	course
Spielen Sie bitte!	You play (the game) now, please.
spielen	to play; to act, perform
A 3 **das Institut, -e**	institute
deutsch	German
leicht	*here:* easy; light, mild
& = und	and
schnell	quick, fast
Was ist denn hier los?	What's going on here?

A 4

Bachmann, Ingeborg (1926–1973)	Hesse, Hermann (1877–1962)
Böll, Heinrich (1917–1985)	Lasker-Schüler, Else (1869–1945)
Goethe, Johann Wolfgang von (1749–1832)	Suttner, Bertha von (1843–1914)
	Wolf, Christa (geb. 1929)
	Zweig, Stefan (1881–1942)

German and Austrian writers

Unterstreichen Sie bitte den Familiennamen!	Please underline the surnames.
unterstreichen	to underline

Deutsche Namen	Vierth, Anna-Maria
Müller, Stefanie	Seelen, Christian von
Weber, Gerda	Richter, Michaela
Klein, Michael	Döhlmann, Heinrich
Schmidt, Heinrich	Fischer, Jens Uwe
Schwarz, Thomas	

Groß, Karl-Heinz *First names are often hyphenated in German.*

Schmidt-Riembach, Susanne *A hyphenated surname.*

A 5 die Anrede, -n	form of address
Frau Richter	Mrs Richter

die Frau, -en	*here:* Mrs; woman; wife
Fräulein Müller	Miss Müller
das Fräulein, -	young lady; Miss

---

die Frau – das Fräulein
Notice that the definite article for Fräulein *is „das". This is because the word is a diminutive (-lein). Normally women are addressed as „Frau" from about 20 years, even if unmarried.*

Herr Schmidt	Mr Schmidt
der Herr, -en	Mr ; master
das Beispiel, -e	example
Und nun Sie!	And now you./You do it now.
nun	now
sprechen* (du sprichst, er spricht)	to speak
A 6 **lesen*** (du liest, er liest)	to read
komisch	*here:* strange; comical, funny
klein	small, little
groß	*here:* tall; large
Was ist denn mit den Namen los?	What is wrong with the names?
	denn = then, *and would not be put in in English.*
mit	with
Antworten Sie bitte!	Please answer.
antworten	to answer
nein	no
A 7 **Auf Wiedersehen!**	Goodbye.
B 1 Wie heißt das auf deutsch?	What is that called in German?
Wer ist denn das?	Who is that?
	Again denn *would not be translated.*
wer	who
Oh!	Oh!
Ich bin Grammatiklehrerin.	I am the grammar teacher.
die Lehrerin, -nen	teacher
die Grammatik, -en	grammar
Fragen Sie bitte!	Please ask.
fragen	to ask
die Tür, -en	door
Warum „die"?	Why „die"?
Warum?	Why?

Der Artikel von „Tür" ist . . .	The article for „Tür" is . . .
der Artikel, -	the article *(in grammar)*
von	*here:* for, of; from; by
femininum (= f)	feminine
Das ist so!	That's that! (there's no argument about it)
das Fenster, -	window
Buchstabieren Sie bitte!	Spell it, please.
buchstabieren	to spell
neutrum (= n)	neuter
Moment bitte, langsam!	Just a moment, please. Go slowly.
der Moment, -e	moment
langsam	slowly
der Stecker, -	electric plug
Ach so!	Oh, I see!/Oh! That's it!
das Buch, ̈er	book
Sprach|brücke	*The name of the book you are learning German from is put together from the words* die Sprache (= the language) *and* die Brücke (= the bridge). *So* Sprachbrücke *means: language is like a bridge of words from country to country, from one people to another.*

B 3	der bestimmte Artikel	the definite article
	der Singular, Singularformen	singular, singular forms
	der Plural, Pluralformen	plural, plural forms
	maskulinum (= m)	masculine
	der Nominativ, -e	the nominative
	der Akkusativ, -e	the accusative
	der Dativ, -e	the dative
	der Genitiv, -e	the genitive
B 4	**die Übung, -en**	exercise
	der Lehrer, - (in f)	teacher
	der Tisch, -e	table
	der unbestimmte Artikel	the indefinite article
	Nom. = Nominativ	nominative
	Akk. = Akkusativ	accusative
	Dat. = Dativ	dative
	Gen. = Genitiv	genitive

B 5	**die Tasche, -n**	bag, handbag
	Ja, richtig.	Yes, that's right.
	richtig (≠ falsch)	right, correct (≠ wrong)
	das Heft, -e	exercise book
B 6	Ein Baum ist ein Baum.	A tree is a tree.
	der Baum, ⁻e	tree
B 7	das Alphabet, -e	alphabet
	das ABC, -s	ABC
	der Umlaut, -e	umlaut (= *vowel modification*)
	Hier entsteht ein Deutschlehrwerk.	A German textbook is being put together here.
	entstehen*	to originate, start; arise
	das Lehrwerk, -e	textbook
B 8	Wie schreibt man das?	How do you write that?
	schreiben*	to write
	man	one, you *or* they *(as indeterminate forms)*
	der Bleistift, -e	pencil
	Groß oder klein?	Large or small? *Here:* With an initial capital or a small letter?
	oder	or
	das Substantiv, -e	noun
	auch	also
	der Nachbar, -n (in f)	neighbour
C 1	**der Beruf, -e**	occupation, job, profession
	Wer macht was?	Who does what?
	machen	*here:* to do; to make
	das Interview, -s	interview
	Herr Dr. Dadu	Dr Dadu *(Do not translate* Herr.)
	Dr. = Doktor	Dr = Doctor

> *Here* **Doktor** *is an academic title. In German it is combined with the name in addressing the person, thus:* Herr Dr. Müller, Frau Dr. Maier. *You only say* "Herr Doktor" *and* "Frau Doktor", *without using the name, when dealing with medical doctors.*

Sie sind hier der Direktor.	You are the director here.
hier	here
der Direktor, -en (in f)	director
Ja also, ich leite das Sprachinstitut.	Yes, well I am the head of the institute.

> *Note:*
> **ich** *is not given an initial capital, unless, of course, it starts a sentence.*

leiten (du leitest, er leitet) — to be head of . . ., to lead, direct, manage

die Sekretärin, -nen — secretary
(der Sekretär, -e)

> **Sekretärin**
> *has been a typically female occupation. The masculine form of the word in German* (Sekretär) *is only used for a higher state official, or for a person in an authorized position in a political party, such as the* Staatssekretär (State Secretary), *or the* Generalsekretär der CDU (General Secretary of the CDU).

Ich telefoniere viel.	I telephone a lot.
telefonieren	to telephone
viel	a lot, much, many
der Dozent, -en (in f)	lecturer
unterrichten	to instruct, teach
der Kollege, -n (Kollegin f)	colleague
Er gibt Kurse für Techniker.	He gives courses for technicians.
geben* (du gibst, er gibt)	to give
für	for
der Techniker, - (in f)	technician
sie unterrichten	they teach
der Anfänger, - (in f)	beginner
zwei Assistenten aus Deutschland	two assistants from Germany
zwei	two
der Assistent, - en (in f)	assistant
aus Deutschland	from Germany
aus	*here:* from; of; out of
Deutschland	Germany
der Konversationskurs, -e	conversation course
Und dann ist da noch Frau Larsen.	And then there is Mrs Larsen.
dann	then
noch	*here:* in addition; still, yet, besides
Sie leitet das Sprachlabor.	She is in charge of the language laboratory.

das Sprachlabor, -s	language laboratory
der Hausmeister, - (in f)	caretaker, janitor
der Student, -en (in f)	student
Ich studiere Biologie.	I am studying biology.
studieren	to study
die Biologie	biology
Ich lerne hier Deutsch.	I am learning German here.
lernen	to learn
C 2 falsch ($\neq$ richtig)	incorrect, wrong ($\neq$ right)
C 3 die Technik, -en	technical science, engineering
C 4 das Personalpronomen, -	personal pronoun
Vergleichen Sie bitte!	Please compare them.
vergleichen	to compare
zum Beispiel	for example
Ergänzen Sie bitte!	Please complete this.
ergänzen	to complete
C 5 Benutzen Sie ein Wörterbuch!	Use a dictionary.
benutzen	to use
das Wörterbuch, ⸚er	dictionary
der Arzt, ⸚ (Ärztin f)	doctor *(of medicine)*
der Landwirt, -e (in f)	farmer *(who owns the property)*
der Fotograf, -en (in f)	photographer
der Geschäftsmann,	businessman
Geschäftsleute	business people
der Verkäufer, -(in f)	salesman/woman; shop assistant
der Architekt, -en (in f)	architect
C 6 die Auskunft, ⸚e	information, particulars, details
Auskunft zur Person	personal particulars/information
die Person, -en	person
Sprechen Sie bitte miteinander!	Please talk to each other.
miteinander	with each other, with one another
Was sind Sie von Beruf?	What is your occupation?
der Beruf, -e	occupation, profession
C 7 vorstellen	to introduce
die Endung, -en	the ending *(of a word)*
die Person, -en *(grammatisch)*	the person *(in grammar)*
1. Person	1st person
2. Person	2nd person
3. Person	3rd person
der Infinitiv, -e	the infinitive
sein	to be
das Verb, -en	verb

1

D 1	**die Frage, -n**	question
	die Entscheidungs‗frage, -n	question requiring a decision (Yes/No question)
	die Antwort, -en	answer
	doch	*an emphatic affirmative to a negative question (eg.* Indeed I am!)
	Das verstehe ich überhaupt nicht.	I don't understand that at all.
	verstehen	to understand
	überhaupt	at all; in general
	nicht	not
	Bitte nicht so kompliziert!	Not so complicated, please.
	kompliziert	complicated
	Bitte wiederholen Sie!	Please repeat.
	wiederholen	to repeat; to revise
	Bitte erklären Sie!	Please explain.
	erklären	to explain
	Gut, . . .	Good . . .
	Wunder/Wander	*German surnames*
	Ralf	*first name for a male*
	Verstehen Sie das jetzt?	Do you understand that now?
	jetzt	now
	Ich glaube ja.	I think so.
	glauben	to think, believe
	ein bißchen	a little
	vielleicht	perhaps
♪1	die Intonation, -en	intonation
	die Satz‗melodie, -n	the rise and fall of the sentence
	Sprechen Sie bitte nach!	Please say this after me. *(or whoever/whatever is giving the pattern)*
	nach‗sprechen* (du sprichst nach, er spricht nach)	to repeat or say after someone
♪2	die Silbe, -n	syllable
	der Wort‗akzent, -e	word stress (syllable stress within a word)
	markieren	to mark
♪3	der Satz‗akzent, -e	sentence stress (word(s) stressed within a sentence)
E	Entschuldigen Sie, . . .	Excuse me . . .
	entschuldigen	to excuse yourself, apologise
	Im Buch steht:	In the book it says . . .
F 1	die Tabelle, -n	table (of tabulated information)

1

die Mutter, ̈	mother
der Vater, ̈	father
die Eltern *(Plural)*	parents
das Kind, -er	child
die Visitenkarte, -n	visiting card
	(The script on the visiting card has been made up.)

F 2 in Deutschland — in Germany

der Junge, -n	boy
das Mädchen, -	girl
die Bundesrepublik Deutschland *(Abkürzung:* BRD)	Federal Republic of Germany *(abbreviation:* BRD)
die Deutsche Demokratische Republik *(Abkürzung:* DDR)	German Democratic Republic *(abbreviation:* DDR)
die Republik, -en	republic

F 3 **suchen** — to look for

das Projekt, -e	project
das Lexikon, Lexika	dictionary
Busch, Wilhelm (1832 – 1908)	*artist (of sketches and drawings) and writer*

2

AS **oben**	above, over
unten	below, under
die Glücks¡zahl, -en	lucky number
die Unglücks¡zahl, -en	unlucky number
Wo bin ich?	Where am I?
A 1 Wo ist was . . .?	Where is what . . .?
links	left, to the left, on the left
rechts	right, to the right, on the right
die Bibliothek, -en	library
die Cafeteria, -s	cafeteria
die Damen¡toilette, -n	ladies' toilet
die Toilette, -n	toilet

> **Wo ist bitte die Toilette?**
> *One normally asks for* die Toilette *(or* das WC*) and not for "the bathroom".*

der Eingang, ⁼e	entrance
der Fahrstuhl, ⁼e	lift, elevator
der Film¡raum, ⁼e	film room
der Raum, ⁼e	room
die Garderobe, -n	cloakroom
der Gebets¡raum, ⁼e	prayer room
die Herren¡toilette, -n	men's toilet
das Informations¡brett, -er	notice-board
die Instituts¡leitung, -en	administration office
die Kasse, -n	cash desk
der Klassen¡raum, ⁼e	classroom
das Lehrer¡zimmer, -	teachers' room
der Not¡ausgang, ⁼e	emergency exit
der Ausgang, ⁼e	exit
der Pausen¡raum, ⁼e	room to spend the breaks in
die Pause, -n	break, interval between lessons
der Raum¡plan ⁼e	room plan
der Plan, ⁼e	plan, diagram, scheme
das Sekretariat, -e	secretary's office
das Telefon, -e	telephone
das WC, -	WC, toilet
die Zeitungs¡ecke, -n	corner where the newspapers are available
die Zeitung, -en	newspaper

A 2 der Keller, - cellar, basement
das Erdgeschoß, Erdgeschosse ground floor

> *Note:* **Erdgeschoß** = ground floor *(British English)*
> = first floor *(American English)*
> **Erster Stock** = first floor *(British English)*
> = second floor *(American English)*
>
> *The floors above are numbered accordingly.*

1. Stock = erster Stock first floor *(Amer:* second floor)
2. Stock = zweiter Stock second floor *(Amer:* third floor)
3. Stock = dritter Stock third floor *(Amer:* fourth floor)
4. Stock = vierter Stock fourth floor *(Amer:* fifth floor)
der Stock, Stockwerke floor, level, storey

A 3 Im zweiten Stock rechts. on the second floor, to the right
Im siebten Himmel! In the seventh heaven!
im vierten Stock on the fourth floor
im dritten Stock on the third floor
im zweiten Stock on the second floor
im ersten Stock on the first floor
im Erdgeschoß on the ground floor
im Keller in the basement

A 4 **die Information, -en** information *(Unlike English, this can be used in the plural form.)*

Gibt es hier keinen Pausenraum? Is there no students' room here?/ . . . leisure room for the breaks?

es gibt *German idiom equivalent to:* There is/are

Das weiß ich leider nicht. I'm sorry, I don't know.
ich weiß I know
leider *here:* I'm sorry, . . .; unfortunately
Pl. = Plural plural
Achtung! Watch out! Look out!
. . . „ein" hat keinen Plural, . . . „ein" does not have a plural, but
aber „kein" hat einen Plural. „kein" has a plural.

A 6 bei uns with us, at home

A 7 **oben** above
unten below
in der Mitte in the middle
die Mitte middle

2

A 8	Schwarz	*German surname; the word means:* black.
	die Haupt‿information, -en	most important/ main information
	Tragen Sie bitte die richtige Zahl ein!	Please enter the correct number here.
	eintragen* (du trägst ein, er trägt ein)	*here:* to enter (in a book, list, etc.); to carry in; to yield
	die Zahl, -en	number
A 9	der Architekten‿wettbewerb, -e	competition for architects
	zeichnen (du zeichnest, er zeichnet)	*here:* design, plan; sketch, draw
	die Klasse, -n	class
	Stellen Sie es in der Klasse vor!	Present it to the class.
B 1	die Kardinal‿zahl, -en	cardinal number(s)
	Zählen Sie bitte weiter!	Please carry on counting.
	zählen	to count
	weiter‿zählen	to count on further
	die Million, -en	million
	römische Zahlen	Roman numerals
	arabische Zahlen	Arabic numerals
B 2	die Haus‿nummer, -n	house number
	die Telefon‿nummer, -n	telephone number
	die Paß‿nummer, -n	passport number
	die Konto‿nummer, -n	account number
	die Kurs‿nummer, -n	number of the course
	die Bibliotheks‿nummer, -n	library number
	die Zimmer‿nummer, -n	room number
	die Personal‿nummer, -n	personal identity number *(In countries where people carry identity cards.)*
	die Steuer‿nummer, -n	tax number *(Each person's personal number on all papers dealing with tax.)*
	die Nummer, -n	number

> *In English the word "number" is used generally, whereas in German* **Zahl** *is used for counting in single or specific numbers (eg. meine Glückszahl = my lucky number) and* **Nummer** *is used for the "whole number" (eg. on a passport, a telephone or a room number).*

Bin ich nur eine Nummer?   Am I only a number?

nur	only
Nach Fritz Werf	According to Fritz Werf
B 3 die Ordinalzahl, -en	ordinal number(s)
der, das, die erste	the first
der, das, die zweite	the second
der, das, die dritte	the third
der, das, die vierte	the fourth
das Sonett, -e	sonnet
die Strophe, -n	verse, stanza
die Zeile, -n	line
das Zimmer, -	room
B 4 Lesen Sie bitte laut!	Please read aloud.
B 5 **Wie viele . . .?**	How many . . .?
Wie viele Klassenräume hat das Sprachinstitut?	How many classrooms has the language institute got?
die Seite, n	*here:* page; side
die Lektion, -en	lesson
B 6 die Glückszahl, -en	lucky number
die Unglückszahl, -en	unlucky number
Das bringt Glück.	That's lucky./That brings good luck.
das Glück	luck
bringen	to bring
Das bringt Unglück.	That's unlucky./That brings bad luck.
das Unglück	bad luck, misfortune; misery
Bei uns ist 13 eine Glückszahl und 7 eine Unglückszahl.	In our country 13 is a lucky number and 7 an unlucky number.
abergläubisch	superstitious
B 7 **der Unterricht**	lesson *(given by the teacher)*
arbeiten (du arbeitest, er arbeitet)	to work
Arbeiten Sie bitte zu zweit!	Please work in twos.
zu zweit	in twos
Können wir auch zu dritt arbeiten?	Can we also work in threes? May we . . .?
können*	to be able to; to know how to; *here:* to be permitted to
zu dritt	in threes
zu viert	in fours
allein	alone
C 1 **das Bild, -er**	picture
Auf Bild 1 steht der Lehrer hinter dem Tisch.	In picture 1 the teacher is standing behind the table.

stehen*	to stand
auf dem Stuhl	on the chair
der Stuhl, ⁼e	chair
hängen*	to hang up, to suspend; to cause to hang (eg. something up)
sitzen* (du sitzt, er sitzt)	to sit
liegen*	to lie, be situated
die Präposition, -en	preposition
lokal	local/locality, position

auf	on, in, at, to
über	over, above, across
in	in, into
neben	near, next to
hinter	behind, after
unter	under (neath), below, among, between
vor	before, in front of
zwischen	between
an	at, in, of, on, to

die Lokalergänzung, -en	complement of location
der Schrank, ⁼e	cupboard
der Cassettenrecorder, -	cassette recorder
der Lichtschalter, -	light switch
der Fußboden, ⁼	floor
die Tafel, -n	board *(for writing on)*, chart, diagram etc. *(in a classroom)*
die Lampe, -n	lamp
die Landkarte, -n	map
dic Cassette, -n	cassette
die Steckdose, -n	wall-socket, electric socket
die Wand, ⁼e	wall
die Ecke, -n	corner
Oh weh!	O-o-oh!, Oh, help! *(cry of sorrow or pain)*
C 2 Beschreiben Sie bitte Ihren Klassenraum!	Please describe your classroom.
beschreiben*	to describe
die Decke, -n	*here:* ceiling; cover

C 4 Wer kann mir helfen? Who can help me?
helfen* (du hilfst, er hilft) to help
Ich finde das Wort nicht. I can't find the word.
finden* ($\neq$ suchen) to find
das Wort, ̈er word
Ach so, vielen Dank! Oh, that's where it is! Thanks very much.

> „**Ach so!**" *is a common expression of recognition or relief.*

---

der Dank, - thanks
C 5 Was steht wo? What is where?
das Grammatikregister, - index of grammar
die Wortliste, -n word list
das Inhaltsverzeichnis, -se the contents, the table of contents
das Verzeichnis, -se the index, register; catalogue, inventory

der Verlag, -e publishing firm
der Autor, -en (in f) author
C 6 unbekannte Wörter unknown words
unbekannt unknown
das Glossar, -e glossary
das Arbeitsbuch, ̈er workbook
C 7 Ist der Platz noch frei? Is the seat/place still free (not occupied)?

der Platz, ̈e place, seat, space
noch still, yet, in addition
frei free *(In the context here:* vacant, unoccupied)

Der ist leider schon besetzt. Unfortunately it is already taken/occupied.

schon already
besetzt occupied
♪ **1** der Laut, -e sound
der Vokal, -e vowel
kurze Vokale short vowel
lange Vokale long vowel
♪ **2** die Wortmelodie intonation within a word
die Melodie, -n melody, rise and fall of the sound line

♪ **3** der Nebenakzent, -e secondary stress
der Hauptakzent, -e main or primary stress

2

D 1 die Satzglied‿stellung — word order in the sentence
der Aussage‿satz, ⸚e — declarative sentence
die W-Frage, -n — *question words beginning with W- (compare English wh-questions)*

der Imperativ‿satz, ⸚e — imperative sentence
nehmen* (du nimmst, er nimmt) — to take

D 2 die Unordnung — disorder, untidiness
ordnen (du ordnest, er ordnet) — to put in order, arrange, organize

E 1 **du** — you *(singular)*
Oh, Entschuldigung! — Oh, excuse me! Oh, I beg your pardon!

die Entschuldigung, -en — apology
ihr — you *(plural)*
wir — we
Warum redet ihr so viel? — Why are you talking so much?
reden (du redest, er redet) — to talk, to speak
Das sagen wir nicht. — We're not saying. We're not telling you.

sagen — to say, tell
wissen* (ich weiß, du weißt, er weiß) — to know *(through knowledge or learning)*

E 3 Machen Sie auch ein Gedicht! — You make up a poem too.
das Gedicht, -e — poem
Und wer hört zu? — And who is listening?
zu‿hören (ich höre zu) — to listen

E 4 **lachen** — to laugh
hihihi hahaha hohoho — *sounds produced when someone laughs*

AS

Mach es wie die Sonnenuhr!	Do what the sundial does.
Zähl die heit'ren Stunden nur!	Only count the bright and cheerful hours.

die Sonnenuhr, -en	sundial
Herzlichen Glückwunsch zum Namenstag!	Best wishes on your name-day!

Namenstag
The day assigned to the Christian saint whose name you share. A tradition in some European countries.

A 1

die Öffnungszeit, -en	opening time(s)
der Montag, -e	Monday
11.00 Uhr	11 o'clock in the morning
der Mittwoch, -e	Wednesday
täglich	daily, every day
von ... bis ...	from ... to ...
der Dienstag, -e	Tuesday
der Stundenplan, ¨e	timetable
die Zeit (-en)	time
die Änderung, -en	alteration, change
Aktuelles	topical events, current events
der Juni	June
ab 15.00 Uhr	from 3 o'clock in the afternoon
das Abschlußfest, -e	farewell party
das Fest, -e	*here:* party; festival
Der Unterricht fällt am Nachmittag aus.	The lesson in the afternoon has been cancelled.
ausfallen* (er fällt aus)	to be cancelled, not take place
am Nachmittag	in the afternoon
der Nachmittag, -e	afternoon
Der Literaturkurs findet heute im Filmraum statt.	The literature course takes place in the film room today.
der Literaturkurs, -e	literature course
heute	today
stattfinden* (er findet statt)	to take place
die Veranstaltung, -en	event, entertainment, function, arrangement

27

der Film‿club, -s   film club

Many foreign words can be written with **c** *or with* **k**, *eg.* der Club/Klub, die Cassette/die Kassette. C *is often used to give the impression that it is about something exclusive or special.*

---

der Mai   May
der Film, -e   film
Der blaue Engel   'The Blue Angel' *(a well-known film starring Marlene Dietrich)*

das Konzert, -e   concert
Mozart, Wolfgang Amadeus   *Austrian composer*
  (1756 – 1791)
Kleine Nachtmusik   'A Little Night Music' *(a work by Mozart)*

der Jazz   jazz
das Theater, -   theatre (*Amer.* theater)
Schiller, Friedrich (1759 – 1805)   *German poet/writer*
Die Räuber   'The Robbers' *(a famous drama by Schiller)*

der Vortrag, ⁻e   lecture
Nürnberg   Nuremberg *(See map inside back cover of textbook.)*

das Fernweh   longing for distant places
der Chor, ⁻e   choir
dienstags   on Tuesdays
der Stamm‿tisch, -e   *table for a group of regular customers in a restaurant, pub, etc.*

jeden Mittwoch   every Wednesday
jeder, jedes, jede   each, every
Café International   *name of a café*
das Café, -s   café
der Brief‿freund, -e (in f)   pen-friend
Bergstraße   *Name of a street:* 'Mountain Road'
der Sport   sport
der Volleyball   volleyball
der Sonnabend, -e   Saturday
der August   August
Deutsche Welle   *the name of a German radio station*
Deutsches Programm   German programme

> *You can receive the German language programmes of* **Deutsche Welle** *throughout the world. You can write to the DW and ask for programme information in your own language. The programme booklet comes out monthly and is free of charge. DW also transmits programmes in 34 different languages.*

das Programmheft, -e	programme booklet
das Programm, -e	programme
kostenlos	free of charge
die Anschrift, -en	address
Abt. (= Abteilung) Hörerpost	the department for listeners' mail
die Abteilung, -en	department
das Postfach, ⁼ er	Post Box
Köln	Cologne *(See map inside back cover of textbook.)*

A 2 **Wann?**   When?
 Um wieviel Uhr?   At what time?
 Um siebzehn Uhr.   At seventeen hours. *That is,* 5 o'clock in the afternoon.
 Wann fängt heute der Unterricht an?   When does the lesson begin today?
 anfangen* (er fängt an)   to begin
 Und um wieviel Uhr ist er zu Ende?   And what time does it finish?
 zu Ende sein   to finish, to come to an end
 das Ende   the end
 Prima, dann kann ich den Film ja sehen.   Good. Then I can certainly see the film./Good. Then of course I can see the film.

> **ja** – *as the answer to a question requiring a decision:*
> Lernt Alli Alga auch Deutsch? – Ja, er lernt auch Deutsch.
> Is Ali Alga also learning German? – <u>Yes,</u> he's learning German too.
>
> **ja** – *as a particle to express confirmation, agreement:*
> Prima, dann kann ich den Film ja sehen.
> Good, then <u>of course</u> I can see the film.

prima	excellent, first class. *Colloquial:* Great! Good!
dann	then

3

	sehen* (du siehst, er sieht)	to see
A 3	**beginnen***	to begin
A 4	Wie spät ist es?	What time is it? (*Literally:* How late is it?)
	spät	late
	Wieviel Uhr ist es?	What time is it?
	Viertel nach neun.	A quarter past nine.
	Wieviel Uhr ist es eigentlich?	What is the exact time?
	eigentlich	proper, real; properly, exactly (*A particle used to ask something definite, certain.*)
	das Viertel	quarter
	nach (*temporal*)	after, past (*in time*)
	die Weltzeit	World Time (*The German expression for: Universal Time Coordinated (UTC), formerly: Greenwich Mean Time (GMT).*)
	Wir bringen den Bericht aus Bonn.	We bring you the Bonn report. (*news commentary on government affairs*)
	bringen* (= senden)	to bring: *here:* to send or transmit
	der Bericht, -e	report, commentary, statement
	Bonn	Bonn (*the Federal Capital; See map inside back cover of textbook.*)
	aus Bonn	from Bonn
	Viertel vor zwölf	a quarter to twelve
	vor (*temporal*)	before, to (*in time*)
	halb elf	half past ten

In English the half hours are expressed as past the last hour, eg. half past ten (o'clock); and in German as halfway to the next hour to come eg. **halb elf** *is halfway on the way to eleven o'clock. Remember that these two are the same time!*

---

halb (*temporal*)	half (*in time – half to go*)
der Tag, -e	day
der Morgen	morning
der Abend, -e	evening
die Nacht, ̈e	night
üben	to practise, exercise
ein Uhr	one o'clock (1 a. m.)

halb eins	half past twelve *(12.30 p. m. The number for the hour coming is ,eins'.)*
A 5 Die Deutsche Welle sendet jetzt Musik von Mozart.	,Deutsche Welle' will now broadcast music by Mozart.
die Uhrzeit	the time *(clock time)*
senden	to broadcast, transmit, send
die Musik	music
Du, mach bitte schnell!	Hurry up, you!
schnell	quick, fast
schnell machen	to do something quickly, to make haste
Dann ist es hier ja schon zwanzig nach acht!	It's already twenty past eight here! *(Here ,dann' would not be trans-lated.)*
schon	already
zwanzig nach acht	twenty past eight
Um halb neun müssen wir wegge-hen!	We have to go at half past eight.
müssen* (ich muß, du mußt, er muß)	must, have to
weggehen* (ich gehe weg)	to go away
A 6 Meine Damen und Herren!	Ladies and gentlemen!
A 7 die Ungeduld	impatience
noch nicht	not yet
Es ist erst Viertel vor.	It is only a quarter to.
erst *(temporal)*	only *(in the sense of time)*
noch lange nicht	not for a long time yet
lange	long
Es ist höchste Zeit!	It's high time! *(ie. that something was done, etc.)*
Eile mit Weile!	*A saying something similar to* "Make haste slowly".
Zeit ist Geld!	Time is money.
Ach was. Immer langsam voran!	So what! Slowly does it. *(These two colloquial English expressions come close to the German.)*
Plumps!	*A sound representing the sense:* to fall.
A 8 Siebenmal	seven times
glücklich	happy
die Lieblingszahl, -en	favourite number

möcht' ich = möchte ich	I would like
ausgeh'n = ausgehen* (ich gehe aus)	to go out
die Woche, -n	week
die Verabredung, -en	*here:* appointment; agreement, arrangement
Wann gehen wir endlich mal zusammen aus?	When are we finally going to go out together?
endlich	at last, finally
mal = einmal	,mal' *in this usage is seldom translated into English.*
zusammen	together
Was schlägst du denn vor, Klaus?	What do you suggest, then, Klaus?
vor̲schlagen* (du schlägst vor, er schlägt vor)	to propose, suggest
Sieh mal hier!	Look here!/Look at this!
sehen* (du siehst, er sieht)	to look, see
heute abend	this evening
Zeit haben	to have time
Montags habe ich immer Sport.	On Mondays I always have sport.
montags	Mondays
immer	always
Schade!	What a pity!
am Dienstag (am = *temporal*)	on Tuesday
Das geht leider auch nicht.	Unfortunately that's no good either.
das geht nicht	that's no good; that's impossible
auch	also; *here:* either
Dienstags gehe ich zum Chor.	On Tuesdays I go to choir-practice.
Hm, . . .	Hm = *a sound representing* 'I see' *or a similar considering expression*
übermorgen	the day after tomorrow
Können wir nicht am Mittwochabend ins Theater gehen?	Can't we go to the theatre on Wednesday evening.
der Mittwoch̲abend, -e	Wednesday evening
ins Theater gehen	to go to the theatre
Aber mittwochs ist doch Stammtisch!	But Wednesday evening is 'regulars' night! *(When the regular customers have a reserved table to themselves.)*
mittwochs	on Wednesdays
Ach ja!	Oh, yes!
der Donnerstag, -e	Thursday

mit|kommen* (ich komme mit) — to come/go with *or* accompany *the person speaking*

Wie dumm! — How stupid!
dumm — stupid
Am Freitag habe ich wieder keine Zeit. — I haven't got any time on Friday, either.
wieder — again; *here:* either
Das finde ich aber wirklich schade! — I think that's really a shame!
Das finde ich schade! — I think that's a shame/a pity!
finden* (= meinen) — to find = *here:* to think
aber — but; *here: a particle that strengthens the expression of regret*

wirklich — really
Und wie ist es am Wochenende? — And how about the weekend?
das Wochen|ende, -n — weekend
Samstags und sonntags bin ich nie hier! — I am never here on Saturdays and Sundays.
samstags — on Saturdays
sonntags — on Sundays

---

montags dienstags mittwochs donnerstags freitags samstags sonntags
When the days of the week are written in German with small initial letters they mean: every Monday, every Tuesday, etc.

---

nie — never
Na, dann bis zum Sankt Nimmerleinstag! — Well, till never-never-day, then! *(Meaning that the speaker does not believe that what they are discussing will ever take place. Nimmer is a contraction of* nie *and* immer.)

bis — till
der Samstag, -e — Saturday
der Sonntag, -e — Sunday
Liebe Bina! — Dear Bina,
lieb — dear; agreeable

Liebe Bina!   Lieber Klaus!   Liebe Eltern!
Dear Bina,   Dear Klaus,   Dear Parents,
Forms of address in letters.

3

A 9 **die Aufgabe, -n**	exercise
die Temporalangabe, -n	time indicator
morgen	tomorrow
der Wochentag, -e	week-day
sonnabends	on Saturdays
die Tageszeit, -en	the times of the day
morgens	in the morning(s)
vormittags	in the morning(s)
nachmittags	in the afternoon(s)
abends	in the evening(s)
nachts	at/by night
der Vormittag, -e	morning *(approx. from ten o'clock to twelve o'clock)*
der Nachmittag, -e	afternoon
in der Nacht	in the night
der Montagmorgen	Monday morning
der Montagvormittag, -e	Monday morning
der Montagnachmittag, -e	Monday afternoon
der Montagabend, -e	Monday evening
heute morgen	this morning
morgen vormittag	tomorrow morning
übermorgen abend	*This is two evenings ahead of now, and in English you would mention the day.*
die Ausnahme, -n	the exception

> Morgen, morgen, nur nicht heute, sagen alle faulen Leute.
> Tomorrow, tomorrow, only not today, all the lazy people say.

---

faul (≠ fleißig)	lazy (≠ diligent)
die Leute *(Plural)*	people
variieren	to vary
der Dialog, -e	dialogue
B 1 Ab wann ist die Bibliothek geöffnet?	What time does the library open?
geöffnet	open
der Anfang, ¨e	the beginning
die Dauer	the duration
Von wann bis wann?	From when till when?

ab wann? |→	from when?
bis wann? →|	till/to when
von wann bis wann? |→|	from when till when?

B 3 **Wie lange?** — How long?

Und wie lange dauert er?	And how long does it last?
dauern *(nur 3. Person)*	to last
zweieinhalb Stunden	two and a half hours
die Stunde, -n	hour
die Minute, -n	minute
die Viertelstunde, -n	quarter of an hour
eine halbe Stunde	half an hour
die Dreiviertelstunde, -n	three quarters of an hour
eineinhalb Stunden (anderthalb Stunden)	one and a half hours
die Uhr, -en	clock, watch
die Muttersprache, -n	mother tongue
Holladrihooo!	*Yodel to try out the echo.*
das Echo, -s	echo

B 4

die Deutschstunde, -n	German lesson
Ding, dong, ding	*The sounds of a bell.*
die Ruhe	quiet, silence
die Konzentration	concentration
Sprechen Sie nach!	Repeat. *(after someone has given the pattern)*
Noch 40 Minuten.	Still 40 minutes./40 minutes to go.
das Datum, Daten	the date, *(pl)* dates; (pl) data
der Termin, -e	time, term; fixed appointment
Wann kommt nur das Ende?	When will the end come?
kommen*	to come
Aahh!	Aah! *(a sound of satisfaction)*
Oh, wie schade!	Oh, what a pity!
Die nächste Deutschstunde beginnt . . .	The next German lesson begins . . .
die Sanduhr, -en	hour glass
Die Zeit verrinnt.	Time's running out.

B 5

die Radiosendung, -en	radio transmission/programme
das Radio, -s	radio
die Sendung, -en	transmission/programme
die Nachrichten	the news

	der Kommentar, -e	commentary
	Weltpolitik aktuell	topical/current world politics
	aktuell	topical, current
	die Weltpolitik	world politics
	der Kulturspiegel	reflections on culture
	die Oper, -n	the opera
	das Wirtschaftspanorama	panorama of the economy
	die Wirtschaft	the economy
	der Sportreport	sports report
	die Presseschau	review of the press
	die Presse	the press
	das Literaturmagazin	literature journal
	die Literatur	literature
	die Volksmusik	folk music
	und so weiter	and so on
	Welche Sendungen hörst Du denn gern?	Which programme do you like to listen to?
	langweilig	boring
	das Thema, Themen	theme, topic, subject, themes
B 6	die Programmvorschau	programme preview
	beantworten (du beantwortest, er beantwortet)	to answer, reply to
B 7	bei Ihnen	with you; *here:* in your region
C 1	Weißt du das genaue Datum?	Do you know the exact date?
	genau *(Adjektiv)*	exact
	Warte mal!	Wait!/Hold on a moment!
	warten (du wartest, er wartet)	to wait
	der Frühling	spring
	der Sommer, -	summer
	der Herbst	autumn, fall *(Amer.)*
	der Winter, -	winter
	das Kursende	the end of the course
	der Monat, -e	month
	der Januar	January
	der Februar	February
	der März	March
	der April	April
	der Juli	July
	der September	September
	der Oktober	October
	der November	November
	der Dezember	December

	das Jahr, -e	year
	die Jahreszeit, -en	the season(s)
C 2	Welches Datum haben wir morgen?	What is the date tomorrow?
	der Sprachkurs, -e	language course
C 3	das Sommerfest, -e	summer festival
	temporal	*(concerning)* time *(grammar)*
	die Jahreszahl, -en	year *(date)*
C 4	Andere Länder – andere Sitten	Other countries – other customs.
	das Land, ⸚er	country
	die Sitte, -n	custom
	Ich habe im Juni Geburtstag.	My birthday is in June.
	der Geburtstag, -e	birthday

> **Der Geburtstag** *is an important day and is celebrated especially by children. The grown-ups celebrate particularly jubilee years like the 30th, 40th, 50th birthdays. The coming of age at 18 is also celebrated.*

Das weiß ich nicht genau.	I don't know exactly.
In meinem Paß steht der 1.1.1965.	In my passport it says . . .
der Paß, Pässe	passport
Bei uns registriert man nämlich nicht das genaue Geburtsdatum.	That is to say, with us the actual date of birth is not registered.
registrieren	to register
das Geburtsdatum, Geburtsdaten	date of birth
Ich bin am 29. Februar 1964 geboren.	I was born on 29 February 1964.
geboren sein am	to be born on
Na, dann feierst du ja nicht oft Geburtstag!	Well, you don't often celebrate your birthday, then!
feiern	to celebrate
oft	often
Das ist nicht so schlimm.	That's not so bad!
schlimm	bad; evil, severe
wichtig	important
der Namenstag, -e	name day
Das möchte ich nicht sagen.	I don't want to tell/say.

> Gregor   Tobias   Edith   Hildegard   Jonas   Moritz   Vinzenz
>
> *Catholic saints. Anyone with a saint's name can celebrate their name day on the saint's day allotted in the calendar. (Catholic Church).*

3

C 6	**der Glückwunsch, ⸚e**	congratulations, best wishes
	Viel Glück!	"Good luck!"
	Alles Gute!	"All the best!"
	Wir gratulieren zum Geburtstag.	Congratulations on your birthday.
	gratulieren	to congratulate
	Zum Geburtstag herzliche Glück-wünsche.	Very best wishes on your birthday.
	herzlich	hearty, cordial
C 7	**der Kalender, -**	calendar
D 1	Moment, ich schlage im Wörterbuch nach.	One moment, I'll look it up in the dictionary.
	nach̠schlagen* (ich schlage nach, er schlägt nach)	to look up, consult
	Aber das paßt nicht.	But that's not suitable./That doesn't fit.
	fallen* (du fällst, er fällt)	to fall
	Dann ist ja alles klar.	Then it's all clear.
	klar	clear
D 3	trennbare Verben	separable verbs
E 1	der Imperativ, -e	the imperative
F 1	Denn ich muß um fünf Uhr beim Arzt sein.	Because I have to be at the doctor's by five o'clock.
	Ja, natürlich.	Yes, of course.
	natürlich	of course, naturally
	Können Sie trotzdem die Aufgaben machen?	Can you do the exercises in spite of that?
	trotzdem	in spite of
	selbstverständlich	of course, naturally
	das Modal̠verb, -en	modal verb
	Achten Sie bitte auf die Endungen!	Pay attention to the endings!
	achten auf (du achtest, er achtet)	to pay attention to, watch out for
	mögen* (ich möchte, du möchtest, er möchte)	to like or care for
G	der Verb̠rahmen, -	verb frames *(concerns the placing of verbs in sentences)*

A 1 Wie groß ist Ihre Familie?
　die Familie, -n
　der Interviewer, - (in f)
　Die Deutsche Welle macht gerade
　　eine Sendung über die Familie.
　gerade *(temporal)*

　Kann ich Ihnen ein paar Fragen stellen?
　eine Frage stellen

　ein paar
　Wir sind sechzehn Personen.

　die Großmutter, ⸚
　der Onkel, -
　die Geschwister *(Plural)*
　der Bruder, ⸚
　die Schwester, -n
　verheiratet
　die Nichte, -n
　der Neffe, -n
　Wir wohnen alle zusammen unter
　　einem Dach.
　wohnen

　alle

　das Dach, ⸚er
　interessant
　Und Sie selbst?
　selbst
　ledig
　Wirklich?
　Bei uns ist das normal.
　normal
　die Durchschnittsfamilie, -n
　der Sohn, ⸚e
　die Tochter, ⸚
　Wie alt sind Sie?
　alt (≠ jung)

How big is your family?
family
interviewer
'Deutsche Welle' is just about to do
　a programme on the family.
just now, straight away, directly
　(in time)
May I ask you a few questions?

to ask a question (of someone), to
　put a question
here: a few
There are sixteen of us. (*ie.* in the
　family)
grandmother
uncle
brothers and sisters
brother
sister
married
niece
nephew
We all live together under one roof.

to live, reside, dwell *(ie. in a house,
　etc.)*
all (collectively, all of them, all the
　family, *etc.*)
roof
interesting
And you yourself?
yourself, myself, himself, *etc.*
unmarried, single
Really?
For us it's quite normal.
normal, usual
the average family
son
daughter
How old are you?
old (≠ young)

Leben Ihre Eltern noch?	Are your parents still living?
leben	to live *(ie. to be alive)*
Mein Vater ist schon tot.	My father is already dead.
tot	dead
geschieden	divorced
Darüber möchte ich nicht sprechen.	I would rather not talk about it.
A 2 der Familienstand	marital status, *or* legal status in a family
verwitwet	widowed
A 3 die Verwandtschaftsbezeichnung, -en	relationships *(in the extended family)*
der Großvater, ̈	grandfather
die Tante, -n	aunt
der Vetter, -n	cousin *(male)*
der Cousin, -s	cousin *(male)*
die Cousine, -n	cousin *(female)*
die Schwiegermutter, ̈	mother-in-law
die Base, -n	cousin *(female)*
der Schwager, ̈	brother-in-law
die Schwägerin, -nen	sister-in-law
die Schwiegertochter, ̈	daughter-in-law
der Schwiegersohn, ̈e	son-in-law
der Enkel, - (in f)	grandchild

das Schema, -s	model, plan; scheme; arrangement
weiblich	feminine
männlich	masculine
Perspektive des Ehemannes	perspective of the husband

die Perspektive, -n	perspective
der Ehe‿mann, ⸚er	husband
der Schwieger‿vater, ⸚	father-in-law
die Ehe‿frau, -en	wife
Übersetzen Sie bitte die Verwandt-schaftsbezeichnungen!	Please translate the family relation-ships (designated in the table).
übersetzen (du übersetzt, er übersetzt)	to translate

A 7 Ich bin mutterseelen‿allein! — I am all alone!

B 1 das Foto‿album, Fotoalben — photograph album

unsere Fotos	our photos
unser	our
das Foto, -s	photo
das Familien‿foto, -s	family photo
Das Foto hier ist aber alt!	This photo here is old! (*Here* aber *helps to express astonishment.*)
Das ist eine Hochzeit im Jahr 1932.	That is a wedding in 1932.
die Hochzeit, -en	wedding
heiraten (du heiratest, er heiratet)	to marry, to get married
die Groß‿tante, -n	great aunt
der Groß‿onkel, -	great uncle
Dort hinten in der zweiten Reihe links . . .	There, at the back, in the second row on the left . . .
dort	there
hinten	behind, at the back
die Reihe, -n	row, line
Sie kommt übrigens aus Frankreich.	By the way, she comes from France.
kommen* aus	to come from (*the place of origin*)
übrigens	*here:* by the way, incidentally; after all; besides
Frankreich	France
Erzählen Sie bitte mehr!	Please tell me/us more.
erzählen	to tell, narrate
das Possessiv‿pronomen, -	possessive pronoun
dein	your (*singular*)
sein	his
euer	your (*plural*)
ihr	her

B 2 Aber mein Wagen ist ganz neu. — But my car is quite new.

der Wagen, -	the car (*shown here in the photo*), truck, van
neu (≠ alt)	new (≠ old)

B 3	der Wortwechsel, -	dispute, exchange of words
B 4	Maria Böhlmann, geb. Gutjahr	Maria Böhlmann, née (= born) Gutjahr
	geb. = geborene	born

Maria, Susanne, Heinrich, Irene, Ilse, Paul, Elli, Karl	*German first names*

---

vorn	in front
Jetzt ist er ja schon lange tot.	He has been dead for a long time now.
schon lange	a long time (already)
fotografieren	to photograph, to take a photo
direkt	directly, right (= exactly)
Richtig, . . .	Right, . . ., That's right, . . .
ganz rechts	at the extreme right
ganz *(Adverb)*	quite *(expressing extremity)*
Kirchliche Trauung	Church wedding
St.-Marien-Kirche (St. = Sankt)	St Mary's Church (St. = Saint)

B 5	die Deklination, -en	declension
B 6	der Computer, -	computer
B 7	der Urgroßvater, ⸚	great grandfather
	die Urgroßmutter, ⸚	great grandmother
	die Großeltern	grandparents
	allesamt	altogether
B 8	Bringen Sie bitte Familienfotos mit!	Please bring the family photos with you.
	mitbringen* (ich bringe mit)	to bring with (you, *etc.*)
	die Zeichnung, -en	drawing
C 1	die Familiengeschichte, -n	the family history
	mit achtzehn Jahren	at the age of eighteen
	Sprachen öffnen eine neue Welt	Languages open up a new world.
	öffnen (du öffnest, er öffnet)	to open
	Er hat einen Brief an seinen Geschäftsfreund geschrieben.	He wrote a letter to a business friend of his.
	der Brief, -e	letter
	schreiben* an	to write to
	der Geschäftsfreund, -e	business friend
	Das war 1931.	That was in 1931.

> **Datum: Jahreszahl**
> *Important rule: Calendar years are given without a preposition. You put in the preposition only when the word* Jahr (year) *is used.*
> Das war 1931. – *That was in 1931.*
> Das war im Jahr 1931. – *That was in the year 1931.*

Rendsburg	*a town in North Germany (See map inside back cover of textbook.)*
das Ausland	foreign countries
im Ausland	abroad
Das war damals ungewöhnlich.	That was unusual at that time.
damals	then, at that time
ungewöhnlich	unusual
der Kaufmann, Kaufleute (Kauffrau)	merchant, shopkeeper, people engaged in selling
Er hatte fünf Kinder.	He had five children.
das Hochzeitsfoto, -s	the wedding photo
Bei der Hochzeit habe ich Karl kennengelernt.	I got to know Charles at the wedding.
kennenlernen	to get to know, to make the acquaintance of
Damals hat alles angefangen.	It all began then.
Liebe auf den ersten Blick	love at first sight
die Liebe	love
der Blick, -e	glance, glimpse, look; view; *here:* sight *(to fit the idiom)*
Wir haben die ganze Nacht getanzt.	We danced the whole night through.
ganz *(Adjektiv)*	whole
tanzen (du tanzt, er tanzt)	to dance
Es war herrlich.	It was wonderful.
herrlich	wonderful, glorious, grand
Im August 1932 haben wir dann schon Verlobung gefeiert.	Then in August 1932 we celebrated our engagement.
die Verlobung, -en	engagement
Karl war aber noch sehr jung.	But Charles was still very young.

jung (≠ alt)	young (≠ old)

---

alt ≠ neu
     ≠ jung
Sachen: Ich habe eine <u>neue</u> Tasche.
              Mein Wagen ist schon <u>alt</u>.
Personen: Seine Freundin ist noch sehr <u>jung</u>.
              Ihre Eltern sind schon <u>alt</u>.
Aber: eine <u>neue</u> Welt
              Er hat eine <u>neue</u> Freundin.
              ein <u>neuer</u> Gedanke

C 2	das Präsens	present tense
	das Präteritum	past tense
	das Perfekt	perfect tense
	die Vergangenheit	past
C 4	das Partizip, Partizipien	participle(s)
	regelmäßig	regular(ly)
C 5	unregelmäßig	irregular(ly)
	der Vokal͜wechsel, -	vowel change
	der Konsonanten͜wechsel, -	consonant change
C 6	Aber das erkläre ich später.	But I will explain that later.
	später	later
C 7	**gestern**	yesterday
	vorgestern	the day before yesterday
C 8	Schreiben Sie bitte ganze Sätze!	Please write whole sentences.
	der Satz, ̈e	sentence *(in this context)*; clause
	der Glücks͜tag, -e	lucky day
C 9	**die Geschichte, -n**	story, history
	Ina	*a girl's first name*
	Es ist ganz einfach	It is quite easy.
	einfach (= leicht)	easy
	Sie lernen nicht mehr allein.	They are no longer learning alone.
	nicht mehr	no longer
D 1	das Kurs͜porträt, -s	portrait of the course
	die Wandzeitung, -en	wall newspaper
	die Zeitung, -en	newspaper
	das Kurs͜foto, -s	course photo
	die Collage, -n	collage
	die Kurs͜zeitung, -en	the course newspaper
	die Karikatur, -en	caricature

Tolle Idee!	A great idea!
toll	terrific! great!
die Idee, -n	idea
Ich bin dagegen.	I'm against it.
Ich habe keine Lust.	I don't want to./I can't be bothered.
Lust haben	to want to do something
die Lust	pleasure, desire, delight
Das macht viel Arbeit.	That will be a lot of work.
die Arbeit, -en	work
die Reportage, -n	eye-witness account, running commentary
zuerst	first, at first
der Zeitplan, ̈e	time chart
die Liste, -n	list
brauchen	to need
der Klebstoff, -e	glue
das Papier	paper
die Schere, -n	scissors
der Fotoapparat, -e	camera
der Apparat, -e	apparatus
♪1 offene Vokale	open vowels
geschlossene Vokale	closed vowels
Ypsilon	Y
das Boot, -e	boat
der Typ, -en	type *(of person)*
♪3 vokalisiertes r	vocalized r
♪4 die Tomate, -n	tomato
die Melone, -n	melon
die Banane, -n	banana
die Zitrone, -n	lemon

45

5

AS Europa	Europe
die Sprachminderheit, -en	minority languages
die Sprachengruppen der Welt	language groups/regions of the world
A 1 Deutsch als Muttersprache	German as mother tongue
als	as
die Muttersprache, -n	mother tongue
Außerdem wird Deutsch in Österreich . . . gesprochen.	German is also spoken in Austria . . .
werden* (Deutsch wird gesprochen.)	to become; to turn out; shall/will *(The future element is included in the becoming.)*
außerdem	in addition, besides, as well as that
Österreich	Austria
Luxemburg	Luxembourg
Liechtenstein	Liechtenstein
in einem Teil der Schweiz	in a part of Switzerland
der Teil, -e	part
die Schweiz	Switzerland
Insgesamt werden in der Schweiz vier Sprachen gesprochen.	Altogether four languages are spoken in Switzerland.
insgesamt	altogether, in total
Französisch	French
Italienisch	Italian
Rätoromanisch	Rhaeto-Romanic *or (more commonly)* Romansch: *from Romance dialects spoken in the Canton of Grisons, and an official language of Switzerland since 1938.*
in einigen Ländern	in some countries
einige	some
die Minderheit, -en	minority
Belgien	Belgium
Italien	Italy
das Passiv	the passive
das Vaterland, ⁻er	fatherland
Deutsche Schriftsteller und ihr Staat seit 1945.	German Writers and Their Country Since 1945.
A 2 Denn dort leben ca. 4,5 Millionen Ausländer.	For about 4.5 million foreigners live there.
denn *(Konjunktor)*	for, because, then
der Ausländer, - (in f)	foreigner

Sie kommen aus der Türkei.	They come from Turkey.
die Türkei	Turkey
Jugoslawien	Yugoslavia
Griechenland	Greece
Spanien	Spain
die Niederlande *(Plural)*	The Netherlands
Portugal	Portugal
Türkisch	Turkish
Serbokroatisch	Serbo-Croatian
Griechisch	Greek
Spanisch	Spanish
Niederländisch	Dutch
Portugiesisch	Portuguese
Woher kommen Sie? –	Where do you come from? –
Aus Portugal.	From Portugal.
Woher?	From where?
der Türke, - (Türkin f)	Turk
der Jugoslawe, -n (Jugoslawin f)	Yugoslav
der Italiener, - (in f)	Italian
der Grieche, -n (Griechin f)	Greek
der Österreicher, - (in f)	Austrian
der Spanier, - (in f)	Spaniard
der Niederländer, - (in f)	Dutchman, Netherlander
der Portugiese, -n (Portugiesin f)	Portuguese

Nationalitätennamen

maskulinum	**femininum**
der Italien**er**	die Italiener**in**
der Koreaner	die Koreaner**in**
der Griech**e**	die Griech**in**
der Türk**e**	die Türk**in**
der Franz**ose**	die Franz**ösin**

Arbeiterwohlfahrt	workers' welfare
Bezirksverband Nordwürttemberg	District Association of North Wurtemberg
Beratungsstelle für jugoslawische Arbeitnehmer	Advisory Office for Yugoslav Employees/Workers
Wege zum Beruf	Ways to a profession/vocational employment

Ich kann nicht richtig Griechisch.	I cannot speak Greek correctly.
Ich kann nicht richtig Deutsch.	I cannot speak German correctly.

A 3

die Auswahl	selection
Anzahl der Sprecher in Millionen	Numbers of speakers in millions
die Anzahl	number
der Sprecher, - (in f)	speaker
Chinesisch	Chinese
Englisch	English
Hindi	Hindi
Russisch	Russian
Arabisch	Arabic
Bengali	Bengali
Japanisch	Japanese
China	China
Großbritannien	Great Britain
die USA *(Plural)*	United States of America
Australien	Australia
Kanada	Canada
Lateinamerika	Latin America
Indien	India
Pakistan	Pakistan
die UdSSR	the USSR – the Union of Socialist Soviet Republics
Ägypten	Egypt
der Libanon	the Lebanon
Bangladesch	Bangladesh
Brasilien	Brazil
Angola	Angola
Japan	Japan

> *In the workbook you can find in the solutions to Lesson 5 a list of almost all the names of countries and languages.*

A 4

der Dialekt, -e	dialect
Bayern	Bavaria
Bayrisch	Bavarian *(dialect)*
Doch, das stimmt.	Yes, that's right.
stimmen	to be correct, right
Frankfurt	Frankfurt
Hessisch	Hessian *(dialect in the German State of Hesse)*

Stuttgart	Stuttgart
Schwäbisch	Swabian *(dialect)*
Norddeutschland	North Germany
Platt deutsch	Low German (a *dialect spoken in North Germany)*
der Frankfurter, - (in f)	person from Frankfurt
der Stuttgarter, - (in f)	person from Stuttgart

Städte und ihre Einwohner		**Towns and their inhabitants**
Stuttgart	der Stuttgar**ter**	die Stuttgarter**in**
Berlin	der Berlin**er**	die Berliner**in**
München	der Münch**ner**	die Münchner**in**
Frankfurt	der Frankfurt**er**	die Frankfurter**in**
Hamburg	der Hamburg**er**	die Hamburger**in**
Plural:	die Hamburg**er**	die Hamburger**innen**

der Bayer, -n (in f)	Bavarian
der Norddeutsche, -n	North German

maskulinum	**femininum**
der Deutsche	die Deutsche
ein Deutsch**er**	eine Deutsche
Plural: die Deutsch**en**	
Deutsch**e**	

Ja, einigermaßen.	Yes, to some extent.
Hochdeutsch	High German
Das wird überall gesprochen.	That is spoken everywhere.
überall	everywhere
Hamburg	Hamburg
München	Munich
Ick snack Platt.	I speak Platt *(the Low German dialect of the north)*.
Isch babbel Hessisch.	I speak Hessish *(the dialect of Hesse)*.
I schwätz Schwäbisch.	I speak Swabian *(the dialect of Swabia)*.
I red Boarisch.	I speak Bavarian.
▲ 6 **die Fremd sprache, -n**	foreign language
die Zweit sprache, -n	second language
der Text, -e	text

49

5

5

Wie viele Menschen . . . lernen Deutsch als Fremdsprache?	How many people . . . learn German as a foreign language?
der Mensch, -en	man, human being, person

B 1 Ich will im Urlaub nach Berlin und Wien fahren. — I intend to go to Berlin and Vienna for my holidays.

wollen* (ich will, du willst, er will) — to want, intend to

der Urlaub — holidays, leave

nach *(lokal)* — to *(a place)*

Berlin — Berlin *(See map inside back cover of textbook.)*

Wien — Vienna

fahren* (du fährst, er fährt) — to travel, go *(with a vehicle)*

Ich möchte gern mit den Menschen reden. — I would like to talk to the people.

gern — *positive expression of willingness:* with pleasure

Ghana — Ghana

Unsere Firma importiert sehr viel aus Deutschland. — Our firm imports a lot from Germany.

die Firma, Firmen — firm(s)

importieren — to import

Ich brauche Deutsch für meine Karriere. — I need German for my career.

die Karriere, -n — career

der Schüler, - (in f) — pupil, student at school

Indonesien — Indonesia

Deutsch ist an meiner Schule ein Pflichtfach. — German is a compulsory subject in my school.

die Schule, -n — school

das Pflichtfach, ̈er — compulsory subject

das Studium, Studien — study at a university or college

der Psychologe, -n (Psychologin f) — psychologist

das Fachbuch, ̈er — text book *(on a specific subject)*

im Original lesen — to read in the original

das Original, -e — the original

Andere Leute haben andere Gründe genannt. — Other people have mentioned other reasons.

die Leute *(Plural)* — people

der Grund, ̈e — reason

nennen* — to name, mention

mit einer Brieffreundin auf deutsch korrespondieren — to correspond in German with a pen-friend

korrespondieren	to correspond, write to
mehr Geld verdienen	to earn more money
das Geld	money
verdienen	to earn
einfach zum Vergnügen	simply for pleasure
das Vergnügen, -	pleasure

B 2 Was ist eigentlich der Unterschied zwischen . . .? — What is the actual difference between . . .?

der Unterschied, -e	difference
Das meine ich nicht.	I don't mean that.
meinen	to mean, think, intend
Sie kann nur Grammatikregeln geben.	She can only give grammatical rules.
die Grammatik‿regel, -n	grammatical rules
die Gebrauchs‿regel, -n	rules of use
die Regel, -n	rule
Vergleicht doch mal die Beispiele!	Well, just compare the examples!
	(Here doch mal *reinforces the idea of doing something for yourself.)*
doch *(Partikel)*	*here:* just, at least
der Wunsch, ⸚e	wish
höflich	polite
Ich möchte Sie etwas fragen.	I would like to ask you something.
etwas	something
der Wille	the determination to do something
die Pflicht, -en	duty
die Vorschrift, -en	rule, instruction
die Fähigkeit, -en	ability
die Möglichkeit, -en	possibility
die Erlaubnis	permission

C 1 Meinungen zur Grammatik — opinions on grammar

die Meinung, -en	opinion
Grammatik allein ist nicht wichtig.	Grammar by itself is not important.
wichtig	important
Dann ist Deutschlernen nicht schwer.	Then it's not difficult to learn German.
schwer (= schwierig; ≠ leicht)	difficult (≠ easy)
Was denken Sie?	What do you think?
denken*	to think
Braucht man Grammatik?	Does one need grammar?
Die Menschen lernen verschieden.	People have different ways of learning.

verschieden	different
Manche lernen intuitiv.	Some learn intuitively.
mancher, manches, manche	some
intuitiv	intuitive(ly)
systematisch	systematic(ally)
alle Regeln	all the rules
Aber jeder muß seine Methode selbst finden.	But everyone must find his own method.
jeder, jedes, jede	each, every
die Methode, -n	method
Ich persönlich finde Grammatik spannend.	I personally find grammar absorbing.
persönlich	personally
spannend	absorbing, gripping; exciting, thrilling
Ach, vergessen Sie die Grammatik!	Oh, forget grammar!
vergessen* (du vergißt, er vergißt)	to forget
Ich finde Grammatik schrecklich.	I find grammar dreadful.
schrecklich	dreadful, terrible
Immer nur Tabellen.	There's always just tables (tabulated information).
Meiner Meinung nach ist Grammatik unnötig.	In my opinion grammar is unnecessary
unnötig	unnecessary
Kommunikation ist alles!	Communication is all that matters!
die Kommunikation	communication
alles	all, everything

---

all-

Wir wohnen <u>alle</u> unter einem Dach. *(pronoun for persons)*
We all live under one roof.

Sie wollen <u>alle</u> Regeln wissen. *(attributive)*
They want to know all the rules.

Kommunikation ist <u>alles</u>! *(pronoun for things)*
Communication is all that matters!

Hauptsache, ich verstehe Sie!	The main thing is that I understand you!
die Hauptsache, -n	the main thing
überflüssig	superfluous
Im Gegenteil!	Quite the opposite!

5

	das Gegenteil, -e	the opposite
	das Skelett, -e	skeleton
	positiv	positive
	negativ	negative
D 1	die Wortstellung, -en	word order
	der Konjunktor, -en	conjunction
♪ 1	der Diphthong, -e	diphthong
♪ 2	der Murmellaut, -e	schwa *(or* shwa*) (The unstressed syllable labelled* [ə] *in the International Phonetic Alphabet, eg. English:* around*)*

Das Interesse für Fremdsprachen ist klein.	There is little interest in foreign languages.
das Interesse (-n)	interest
fremd	foreign
die Brücke, -n	bridge

E 1 die Barriere, -n — barrier

Sprachenlernen ist mein Hobby.	Learning languages is my hobby.
das Hobby, -s	hobby
der Traum, ⁻e	dream
Keine Mißverständnisse mehr . . .!	No more misunderstandings . . .!
das Mißverständnis, -se	misunderstanding
kein . . . mehr	no more / no longer
der Krieg, -e	war
Ich bin erwachsen.	I am grown-up.
Ich kann meine Gedanken ausdrücken.	I can express my thoughts.
der Gedanke, -n	thought
ausdrücken (ich drücke aus)	to express
über komplizierte Sachen sprechen	to talk about complicated things
sprechen* über	to speak / talk about
die Sache, -n	thing
Doch Deutsch spreche ich wie ein Kind.	But I speak German like a child.
doch *(Konjunktor)*	but, however, for all that, still
unsicher	uncertain
die Angst, ⁻e	fear, anxiety
Angst haben	to be afraid
der Grammatikfehler, -	grammar mistakes
der Fehler, -	mistake
Na und?	So what?
Meine Aussprache ist komisch.	My pronunciation is funny.

die Aussprache	pronunciation
Das macht nichts!	That doesn't matter.
nichts	nothing
das Abenteuer, -	adventure
Das macht Spaß.	It's fun.
der Spaß, Späße	fun
Diskutieren Sie bitte in Ihrer Muttersprache!	Please discuss it in your mother tongue.
diskutieren	to discuss

AS Willkommensgruß nach
  Landessitte
die Begrüßung
hochsprachl. = hochsprachlich von
  „Hochsprache"

customary national greeting of welcome
greeting
standard educated speech *(The pro-
  nunciation, vocabulary and grammar use representing the most
  respected form of a cultured
  language.)*

flektiert
fliederfarben
violett
der Flieder
die Fliederblütenfarbe
arab. = arabisch
pers. = persisch
ind. = indisch
schwärzlich
Jetzt ganz modisch: lila

inflected
lilac colour
violet
lilac; elder
colour of lilac flowers
Arabic
Persian
Indian
blackish, darkish
Now quite fashionable: lilac

A 1 **das Flugzeug, -e**
  Vor der Ankunft in Lilaland.
  die Ankunft
  der Papa, -s
  Sag mal, . . .
  sagen
  Sehen die Lilaländer genauso aus
    wie wir?
  aus|sehen* (du siehst aus, er sieht
    aus)
  genauso
  wie *(Vergleich)*
  nee = nein
  Die haben sicher nicht so blonde
    Haare wie die Deutschen.
  sicher (= bestimmt)
  blond
  Du bist doch auch nicht blond.
  doch *(Partikel)*

aircraft, plane
Before arrival in Lilaland.
arrival
Dad, Daddy
Tell me, . . .
to tell, to say
Do the people of Lilaland look just
  like us?
to look, to appear, to seem

exactly, precisely
as, like
no
I'm sure they haven't got such fair
  hair as Germans.
sure, certain(ly)
fair, blond(e)
But you aren't blond(e) either.
but; *particle reinforcing the opposite
  of what was said*

6

Tja, . . .	*a sound, here: of resignation*
Da hast du auch wieder recht.	You are right again.
recht haben	to be right
Sind die Lilaländer genauso angezogen wie wir?	Are the people of Lilaland dressed exactly like us?
an̲ziehen* (ich ziehe an)	to dress, to put on clothes; to draw, pull
angezogen sein (ich bin angezogen)	to be dressed
die Mama, -s	Mum, Mummy
Sie tragen nur lila Kleidung.	They only wear lilac-coloured clothing.
tragen* (du trägst, er trägt)	to wear; to bear, carry
die Kleidung	clothing
das Hemd, -en	shirt
die Bluse, -n	blouse
Die Männer tragen manchmal lila Röcke.	The men sometimes wear lilac-coloured skirts.
der Mann, ¨er	man; husband
manchmal	sometimes
der Rock, ¨e	skirt
Soso.	*Here* soso *is a vague expression of agreement like:* That's right.
kaufen	to buy
Das kommt überhaupt nicht in Frage.	That's quite out of the question.
in Frage kommen*	to be possible
Warum denn nicht?	Why not?
Wieso?	But why?
Die sind eben anders als wir.	They are just different from us.
anders als	different from

Jetzt sei doch endlich mal ruhig!	Now just be quiet!
Sei ruhig!	Be quiet!
ruhig	quiet
Warum ist der Vater denn so gereizt?	Why is the father so irritated?
gereizt sein	to be irritated
Der Sohn widerlegt seine Vorurteile.	The son is refuting his prejudices.
widerlegen	to refute, to prove wrong
das Vorurteil, -e	prejudice
Und das ärgert ihn.	And that annoys him.
ärgern	to annoy
an‿kreuzen (ich kreuze an)	to put a cross
A 2 die Damen‿kleidung	women's clothing
die Herren‿kleidung	men's clothing

> *In German people often use **Dame** and **Herr** instead of Frau and Mann.*
> *This is a more polite form of expression.*
> *In public toilets and in restaurants "Damen" and "Herren" are on the respective doors.*

das Kleidungsstück, -e	garment
der Handschuh, -e	glove
die Hose, -n	trousers
der Hut, ⁻e	hat
die Jacke, -n	jacket
der Mantel, ⁻	coat
der Pullover, -	pullover, sweater
der Schuh, -e	shoe
der Strumpf, ⁻e	stocking, sock
das Kleid, -er	garment, dress, (pl) clothes
der Anzug ⁻e	suit
die Krawatte, -n	tie
außereuropäisch	*here:* non-European *(meaning outside of Europe)*
Die bezeichnet man mit dem Fremd-wort.	They are designated by the foreign word.
bezeichnen	to designate, mark, label; to describe
das Fremd‿wort, ⁻er	foreign word
der Sari, -s	sari
der Poncho, -s	poncho
der Kaftan, -e	caftan/kaftan

6

der Kimono, -s	kimono
Machen Sie bitte weiter!	Please go on.
weiter̠machen	to carry on, go on

A 3   die Mode̠frage, -n   question of fashion

      die Mode, -n   fashion

      Möchten Sie so eine Hose tragen?   Would you like to wear trousers like these?

      so ein (m, n), **so eine**   such, such a; like this/these

      Die finde ich schön.   I think they're fine.

      schön   fine, beautiful, handsome

A 4   **die Farbe, -n**   the colour

      hell -   light *(in colour)*

      dunkel -   dark *(in colour)*

      rot   red

      grün   green

      blau   blue

      gelb   yellow

      braun   brown

      grau   grey

      schwarz   black

      weiß   white

      bunt   *here:* multi-coloured; colourful; coloured

      diese Farbe   this colour

      dieser, dieses, diese   this

A 5   **das Spiel, -e**   game

      Ich seh' was!   I see something! (*A game similar to the English one called:* "*I spy with my little eye . . .*")

      (seh' = sehe)

      was = etwas   something

A 7

Sie sind grün

Fahr mit mir den Fluß hinunter	Journey with me down the river
in ein unbekanntes Land,	into an unknown land,
denn dort wirst du Leute sehen,	for you will see people there
die bis heute unbekannt.	who until today are unknown.
Sie sind nett und freundlich,	They are nice and friendly,
doch sie sehen etwas anders aus	though they lock somewhat
als die Leute, die du kennst	different than the people
bei dir zu Haus.	you know at home.

Sie sind grün.	They are green.
Und wenn wir vorübergehn,	And when we pass by
dann tu bitte so, als hättest du die Farbe nicht gesehn.	then please behave as though you had not noticed their colour.
Sie sind grün.	They are green.
Und sie glauben fest daran,	And they firmly believe
daß die Farbe der Haut nichts über uns sagen kann.	that the colour of the skin says nothing at all about people.

der Fluß, Flüsse	river
freundlich	friendly
die Haut	skin
B 1 **das Reisebüro, -s**	the travel office/agency
Atlas *(Name des Reisebüros)*	'Atlas' *is the name of the travel office.*
die Zentrale, -n	the main or central office
örtliche Reiseleitung	regional tours management/organization
örtlich	regional, local
die Reiseleitung, -en	tours management
Name der Familie	name of the family
Vorname des Mannes	first name of the husband
Vorname der Frau	first name of the wife
Vorname(n) des Kindes/der Kinder	first name(s) of the child/children
das Alter, -	age
der Touristikeinkäufer, - (in f)	salesman for tourism
der Journalist, -en (in f)	journalist
besondere Hinweise	special advice
der Hinweis, -e	reference, hint, directive; *here:* advice or information
das Reiseziel, -e	destination
der Tourist, -en (in f)	tourist
Herr Tossu vom Wirtschaftsministerium	Mr Tossu of the Ministry of Economics
das Ministerium, Ministerien	the Ministry
ein Gespräch vermitteln	arrange an interview, mediate or negotiate for a discussion
das Gespräch, -e	conversation, interview, discussion

B 2	Aus zwei mach eins!	One made from two!
	die Leitung, -en	management; leadership
	die Reise, -n	the tour
	das Ziel, -e	destination
B 3	der Reiseleiter, - (in f)	tour leader/manager
	der Leiter, - (in f)	leader, manager
	das Haus, ̈er	house
B 4	das Fragepronomen, -	interrogative pronoun
	Wessen . . .?	Whose . . .?
C 1	**der Beamte, -n** (Beamtin f)	official *(employee of government)*; *here:* Customs officer
	die Paßkontrolle, -n	passport control
	die Kontrolle, -n	control
	die Uniform, -en	uniform
	Und ihre Kollegen beim Zoll sind auch lila gekleidet.	And their colleagues in the Customs are also dressed in lilac.
	der Zoll	Customs
	kleiden	to dress, to clothe
	gekleidet sein	to be dressed
	Er stößt seinen Vater an.	He nudged his father.
	anstoßen* (du stößt an, er stößt an)	to knock, strike against; *here:* to nudge
	So ein komisches Land!	Such a funny country!
	komisch	funny, comical
	meinen	to think, to have the opinion
	Beate schüttelt den Kopf.	Beate shakes her head.
		(In German the definite article den *is used, whereas in English it is* 'her head'.)
	schütteln	to shake
	der Kopf, ̈e	head

den Kopf schütteln	*movement of the head from right to left. That means "no".*
mit dem Kopf nicken	*movement of the head up and down. That means "yes".*

Das finde ich gar nicht.	I don't think so.
gar nicht	not at all, nothing at all
Seht euch doch mal selbst an!	Just look at yourselves!

6

sich an‚sehen* (du siehst dich an, er sieht sich an)	to look at or consider oneself
blau-weiß	blue and white
graublau	greyish blue
der Regenmantel, ∸	raincoat
an‚haben* (du hast an, er hat an)	to wear, to have on, to be dressed in
Außerdem habt ihr auch noch blaue Augen.	Apart from that you have blue eyes.
das Auge, -n	eye
da hinten	back there
Der ist auch ganz in Blau.	He is also completely in blue.
Alle Klingers . . .	All the Klingers . . .
Der Gedanke ist zu komisch!	The thought is so funny!
Da kommt eine Dame auf sie zu.	A woman comes towards them.
zu‚kommen* auf	to come towards
die Dame, -n	woman, lady
Herzlich willkommen!	A very warm welcome!
das Wortfeld, -er	word field
C 2 die Adjektiv‚deklination, -en	declension of adjectives
die Signal‚endung, -en	the ending of the word which signals the case
die Nominal‚gruppe, -n	nominal or noun group
das Adjektiv, -e	adjective
C 3 durch eine lila Brille	through lilac-coloured glasses
durch	through
die Brille, -n	glasses, spectacles
kontrollieren	to control
Aha!	Aha!
deklinieren	to decline *(here: grammatically)*
die Adjektiv‚endung, -en	the adjective ending
ohne	without
Ich sehe schwarz!	I see black! *(a pessimist)*
schwarz‚sehen* (du siehst schwarz, er sieht schwarz)	to see black *ie.* to be a pessimist
rosa	pink, rose-coloured
optimistisch	optimistic
C 4 **Was für . . .?**	What sort of . . .?
C 5 Nichts anzuziehen	Nothing to put on./Nothing to wear.
eine halbe Stunde lang	half an hour long
der Kleiderschrank, ∸e	wardrobe
Jedes Kleid erinnert mich an einen Mann.	Each dress reminds me of a man.

6

erinnern an	to remind of
C 6 die Moden͜schau, -en	fashion show
dreimal	three times
Kleidungsstücke für den Herrn/für die Dame	clothes for the gentleman/for the lady
D 1 die Farben͜symbolik	symbolism of colour
Weiß ist die Farbe der Unschuld.	White is the colour of innocence.
die Unschuld	innocence
die Trauer	grief, mourning
die Treue	loyalty, faithfulness
der Neid	envy, jealousy
die Hoffnung, -en	hope
Nach dtv-Lexikon (dtv = Deutscher Taschenbuch Verlag)	According to the dtv-Dictionary
das Lexikon, Lexika	dictionary
Bei uns bedeutet Gelb nichts.	With us yellow doesn't signify anything.
bedeuten	to mean, to signify
D 2 die Farb͜assoziation, -en	association of colours
Bei dem Wort „Sommer" denke ich an . . .	The word "summer" makes me think of . . .
denken* an	to think of *or* about
farbig	coloured
D 3 die Lieblings͜farbe, -n	favourite colour
D 4 der Maler, - (in f)	painter
der Koch, ⁼e (Köchin f)	cook
das Fechten	fencing *(sport with swords)*
das Judo	Judo
die Religion, -en	religion
die Kommunion, -en	Communion *(A religious festival in the Catholic Church. At the age of 8 or 9 years children are allowed to take part for the first time in the Eucharist.)*
die Taufe, -n	baptism, christening *(Church celebration of reception into the Christian Church.)*
E 1 Grammatik mit Herz	Grammar with love/from the heart *(In* Sprachbrücke *this heading describes grammar texts which also appeal to the emotions.)*

das Herz, -en	heart
die Akkusativ‿ergänzung, -en	accusative complement
die Dativ‿ergänzung, -en	dative complement
Ich sehe nur dich.	I see only you.
Ich höre dir zu.	I listen to you.
Du zeigst mir das Heft.	You show me the exercise book.
zeigen	to show
Wen?	Who? *accusative*
Wem?	Who . . . to? *dative*
Den Genitiv braucht man fast nie!	The genitive is hardly ever required.
fast	almost (fast nie = almost never, *ie.* hardly ever)

F 1 Sagen Sie ruhig „Frau"! — Feel free to use "Frau".
anstrengend — strenuous, tiring
Das glaube ich gern. — I can well believe that.
glauben — to believe, to think
Ich bringe Sie jetzt zu Ihrem Hotel. — I'm taking you to the hotel now.
bringen* — to bring (*towards you; but* 'to take' *in other directions*)

das Hotel, -s — hotel
Unterwegs kann ich Ihnen gleich das Tourismusbüro zeigen. — I can show you the Tourist Office now on the way.
unterwegs — on the way
gleich — equal; alike; *here:* straight away, at once, right away

das Tourismus‿büro, -s — Tourist Office
Da bekommen Sie dann alle weiteren Informationen. — You will get all the additional information there, then.
bekommen — to get
weitere — further
Das ist sehr nett von Ihnen! — That's very nice of you!
nett — nice

F 2 das Kongreß‿büro, -s — Office of the Congress
das Messe‿büro, -s — Trade Fair Office
das Kongreß‿zentrum, Kongreßzentren — Congress Centre
das Stadion, Stadien — stadium
die Messe, -n — Trade Fair

F 3 die Begrüßungs‿form, -en — forms of greeting
So begrüßt man sich in Deutschland. — This is how you greet people in Germany.
sich begrüßen — to greet

sich verbeugen	to bow
Sie nickt mit dem Kopf.	She nods her head.
nicken	to nod
Sie geben sich die Hand.	They shake hands.
die Hand, ⸚e	hand
d. h. = das heißt	that is, that means
Die Dame verbeugt sich nicht so tief wie der Herr.	The lady doesn't bow as deeply as the man.
sich umarmen	to embrace
küssen (du küßt, er küßt)	to kiss
sich küssen	to kiss one another
Sie legen die Hände zusammen.	they put their hands together.
Sie verbeugen sich leicht.	They give a slight bow.
leicht	light, easy; *here:* slight
Er küßt ihr die Hand.	He kisses her hand.
Er wirft sich auf den Boden.	He throws himself down on the floor.
werfen* (ich werfe, du wirfst)	to throw
der Boden, ⸚	floor
reflexive Verben	reflexive verbs
reziproke Verben	reciprocal verbs
F 4 das Begrüßungstheater	Theatre of Welcome

Begrüßungstheater

This is a creation of the authors of this book. You will not find it in a dictionary. In German you can spontaneously build an exact word for a certain situation when you want to express something definite. Journalists often do that. Many of these words only exist for a specific purpose. Especially successful creations make an impression and in the end are used by everyone, so that they find their way into the dictionaries (neologisms).

---

das Hotelzimmer, -	hotel room
international	international
der Europäer, - (in f)	European
Du verbeugst dich tiefer als die Dame.	You bow deeper than the lady.
wie in alten Zeiten	as in olden times
Das mache ich nicht mit.	I'm not going to take part in that.
mitmachen	to take part, to join in

F 5	das Auslandsgeschäft, -e	foreign business, business overseas
	erfolgreich	successful
	Thailand	Thailand
	Arabien	Arabia
	die Anzeige, -n	announcement, advertisement
F 6	die Prozentzahl, -en	percentage
	das Händeschütteln	handshake
	(sich) die Hände schütteln	to shake hands
	dafür (dafür sein)	for (*as opposed to* against); (to be) for that
	insgesamt	all together
	der Gegner, - (in f)	opponent
	unangenehm	unpleasant
	der Befürworter, - (in f)	supporter
♪ 1	Wilhelm	William
	das Clubhaus, -häuser	clubhouse
♪ 2	der Knacklaut, -e	glottal stop
	Albert	Albert
	Amerika	America
	beenden	to finish, to end
♪ 3	der Konsonant, -en	consonant
	der Buchstabe, -n	letter *(of the alphabet)*

7

AS

Die Ameisen	The Ants
In Hamburg lebten zwei Ameisen,	In Hamburg there lived two ants
Die wollten nach Australien reisen.	Who wanted to travel to Australia.
Bei Altona auf der Chaussee	Near Altona on the Chaussee
Da taten ihnen die Beine weh.	They got pains in their legs.
Und da verzichteten sie weise	And there they wisely gave up
Dann auf den letzten Teil der Reise.	The last part of the journey.

Altona	*part of the City of Hamburg*

Norden, Süden, Osten, Westen,	North, South, East, West,
zu Hause ist's am besten.	Home it is that is the best.

A 1

der Tourismus	tourism
das Gespräch, -e	conversation
der Regierungsbeamte, -n (Regierungsbeamtin f)	government official
das Urlaubsparadies, -e	holiday paradise
das ideale Reiseziel	the ideal travel destination
ideal	ideal
Die richtige Medizin gegen unseren grauen Alltag.	The right medicine/The antidote for the daily grind. *(In German medicine is 'against' (gegen) the illness, not 'for' it.)*
die Medizin	medicine
der Alltag	the daily round/grind
der Wald, ⸚er	wood, forest
das Meer, -e	sea
der Strand, ⸚e	beach
die hohen Berge	high mountains
hoch	high
der Berg, -e	mountain, hill
die frische Luft	fresh air
frisch	fresh
die Luft	air
die Kultur, -en	culture, civilization
berühmt	famous
der Tempel, -	temple

Das wollen die deutschen Touristen erleben, genau das!	That's what the German tourists want to experience, just that!
erleben	to experience
Ich freue mich, daß Ihnen mein Land gefällt.	I am very pleased that you like my country.
sich freuen	to be pleased/glad
gefallen* (du gefällst, er gefällt) + *Dativ*	to please
die Sonne, -n	sun
die Wärme	warmth
die Gastfreundschaft	friendliness towards visitors
die Freundschaft, -en	friendship
etwas sympathisch finden	to take a liking to something
sympathisch	nice, pleasant
Genau.	Exactly.
das Wetter	weather
die Landschaft, -en	landscape
phantastisch	fantastic
das Touristikprogramm, -e	programme for the tourists
die Werbung	advertising
Dann kommen gleich doppelt so viele Leute wie im letzten Jahr.	Then twice as many people will come as last year.
doppelt	double, twice
der, das, die letzte	last
Ich fürchte, das gibt Probleme.	I'm afraid that will cause problems.
fürchten	to fear, be afraid
das Problem, -e	problem
die Mentalität, -en	mentality
der Vorteil, -e	advantage
Das können Sie gut brauchen.	You can use that.
A 2 **der Nachteil, -e**	disadvantage
die Devisen *(Plural)*	foreign exchange
Das schon, aber von dem Geld profitieren meistens nur wenige.	That's true, but mostly only a few people profit from the money.
profitieren	to profit
meistens	mostly, generally
wenige	a few, few
Und das zerstört das soziale Klima.	And that destroys the social climate.
zerstören	to destroy, ruin
sozial	social
das Klima, -s	climate
Tourismus schafft viele Konflikte.	Tourism creates many conflicts.

schaffen*   *here:* to create; produce

> **schaffen, schuf, geschaffen**
> *Irregular verb, but present tense without vowel change:* Der Tourismus schafft Konflikte.

der Konflikt, -e	conflict
schockierend	shocking, outrageous
der Kontakt, -e	contact

> **bringen**
> Ich bringe Sie jetzt zu Ihrem Hotel.   I am taking you to your hotel now.
>
> Die Touristen bringen viel Geld.   Tourists bring a lot of money.
> Tourismus bringt Vorteile.   Tourism brings advantages.

Unser Land braucht Arbeitsplätze.	Our country needs jobs.
der Arbeits‚platz, ⸚e	job, vacancy
Tourismus löst unsere wirtschaftlichen Probleme.	Tourism solves our economic problems.
lösen	*here:* to solve; to loosen, to detach
wirtschaftlich	economic
Da bin ich skeptisch.	I'm sceptical about that.
skeptisch	sceptical
die Straße, -n	street, road

> **Straße** *is used in German for both urban and rural areas.*

Die Autos machen unsere Natur kaputt.	The cars are destroying nature/our countryside.
das Auto, -s	car
die Natur	nature
kaputt‚machen	to destroy, to break up
kaputt	broken, damaged
Ich bin für . . ., denn	I am for . . ., because
Ich bin gegen . . ., denn	I am against . . ., because
für etwas sein ≠ gegen etwas sein	to be for something ≠ to be against something

A 3 das Urlaubsland, ⸚er — country for a holiday

B 1 Frau Klinger nimmt einen Schluck Wasser. — Frau Klinger takes a drink of water.

der Schluck, -e — a drop, draught, gulp

das Wasser — water

Dann fährt sie fort. — Then she goes on.

fort‌fahren* (du fährst fort, er fährt fort) — to go on, continue

Ich habe bisher über die Arbeitswelt gesprochen. — I have been speaking about the working world up to now.

bisher — to now, so far

die Arbeits‌welt, -en — the working world

Wir haben gesehen, daß viele Deutsche Fernweh haben, weil ihr Alltag eintönig ist. — We have seen that many Germans have wanderlust because their everyday lives are monotonous.

weil — because

eintönig — monotonous

Es ist ja bekannt, daß . . . — It is well-known that . . .

bekannt — known

Mitteleuropa — Central Europe

wechselhaft — changeable

das Dia, -s — slide, transparency

der Hauptmarkt — the main market place *(Square in Nuremberg. The famous* Christkindlmarkt - 'Christchild' market *is held there at Christmas time).*

der Markt, ⸚e — market

Die Sonne scheint. — The sun is shining.

scheinen* *(i. d. Bed. nur 3. Person Sg. und Pl.)* — to shine

der Himmel, - — heaven, sky

wolkenlos — cloudless

Es weht ein starker Wind. — A strong wind is blowing.

wehen *(nur 3. Person Sg. und Pl.)* — to blow

stark — strong

der Wind, -e — wind

der, das , die gleiche — the same

die Szene, -n — scene

7

Am Himmel sehen Sie dunkle Gewitterwolken.	In the sky you can see dark thunderclouds.

> Der Himmel ist dunk**el**.
> Dort sieht man dunk**le** Gewitterwolken.
> Sie trägt einen dunk**len** Mantel.

die Gewitterwolke, -n	thundercloud, storm cloud
das Gewitter, -	thunderstorm
die Wolke, -n	cloud
Es blitzt und donnert.	There's lightning and thunder. *(The verbs are nominalized in English)*.
blitzen *(unpersönlich)*	to flash lightning
donnern *(unpersönlich)*	to thunder
Schon fallen die ersten Regentropfen.	The first raindrops are already falling.
der Regentropfen, -	raindrop
der Regen, -	rain
der Tropfen, -	drop
Es regnet nicht mehr.	It's not raining any longer.
regnen	to rain
es regnet *(unpersönlich)*	it's raining
Die Straßen sind noch nicht wieder trocken.	The streets are not yet dry again.
wieder	again
trocken	dry
bewölkt	cloudy, overcast
Es ist ziemlich kühl.	It's rather cool.
ziemlich	rather
kühl	cool
Dieser schnelle Wetterwechsel ist typisch für den April.	This rapid change in the weather is typical for April.
der Wetterwechsel, -	change in the weather
typisch	typical
Manchmal schneit es sogar noch.	Sometimes it even snows.
schneien	to snow
es schneit *(unpersönlich)*	it's snowing, it snows

Wetter

unpersönliche Wendungen	*impersonal uses*
es schneit	it's snowing
es regnet	it's raining
es blitzt	there's lightning
es donnert	there's thunder

sogar — even
sich ändern — to change
Der Winter bei uns ist lang, dunkel und kalt. — At home the winter is long, dark and cold.
lang *(temporal)* — long
kalt — cold
Dann steigt bei uns das Reisefieber. — Then we get itchy feet. *(The longing to get away somewhere).*

steigen* — to rise, to mount, climb
das Reisefieber — the strong wish to travel away somewhere

reisen — to travel
der Süden — the south
nicht soviel Sonne — not so much sun
soviel — so much
zum Schluß — finally, in conclusion
der Schluß — the conclusion, end, closing
kurz — *here:* in brief; short
die Bevölkerungsdichte — population density
die Bevölkerung, -en — population
erwähnen — to mention
der Quadratkilometer, - — square kilometre
der Kilometer, - — kilometre
Es ist also kein Wunder, daß wir Fernweh bekommen. — So it's no wonder that we get a longing for distant places.
das Wunder, - — wonder; miracle
Darum ziehen viele Leute, wenn sie Urlaub haben, in die weite Welt hinaus. — For that reason many people move out into the wide world when they have holidays.
darum — for that reason, that's why
hinausziehen* — go out, march out; draw out, prolong

wenn *(temporal)* — when

Wann? – wenn
1. Fragewort: <u>Wann</u> beginnt der Unterricht?

<u>When</u> does the lesson begin?

2. Subjunktor: Viele Leute ziehen in die weite Welt hinaus, <u>wenn</u> sie Urlaub haben.

Many people move out into the wide world <u>when</u> they have holidays.

weit	wide, far off
die Welt, -en	the world

April, April
kann machen, was er will.

April, April
can do what it wants.

der Regenbogen, ⸚	rainbow
schauen	to look at, see
orange	orange
Hab' Sonne im Herzen!	Let the sun into your heart!
Hab' = Habe	have *(here: imperative form)*
Oje, es regnet schon wieder!	Oh, dear! It's raining again!
Besucht Deutschland!	Visit Germany!
besuchen	to visit

B 2 **der Schnee** — snow
die Trockenheit — dryness
die Kälte — the cold
windig — windy
sonnig — sunny

B 3 **der Wetter︠bericht, -e** — weather report
die Wetter︠karte, -n — weather chart
Stockholm — Stockholm

B 5 **der Norden** — north
der Osten — east
der Westen — west
die Direktiv︠ergänzung, -en — complement showing direction
bleiben* — to remain
der Zahn︠arzt, Zahnärzte — dentist
  (Zahnärztin f)
Wohin? — Where (to)?
fliegen* — to fly

B 6

die Reiselust	the love of travel
die Wanderlust	the love of roaming, wanderlust
der Biologenkongreß	biologists' congress
der Kongreß, Kongresse	congress
Das Wandern ist des Müllers Lust . . .	Roaming is the Miller's joy . . . *(the beginning of a roaming song)*
wandern	to roam, rove, go hiking
der Müller, -	miller
Mein Vater war ein Wandersmann . . .	My father was a roaming man . . . *(the beginning of a roaming song)*

Wandern

This is a typical German leisure-time activity. They climb high mountains, or walk for many hours through the natural countryside to a specific destination. Real hikers wear strong walking shoes and a rucksack on their backs. There are many hiking songs which are sung when out roaming.

B 7

das Reisegeld	travelling expenses
die Statistik, -en	statistic
die Reiseausgabe, -n	expenditure on travel
Dänemark	Denmark
England	England
DM = Deutsche Mark	German Mark (West)
die Milliarde, -n	milliard, a thousand million

C 1

Deins ist mir einerlei. (Das ist mir einerlei.)	That's all the same to me.
pronominal	pronominal
die Form, -en	form

C 2

das Hotelzimmer, -	hotel room

D 1

der Nebensatz, ̈e	subordinate clause
der Hauptsatz, ̈e	main clause
der Subjunktor, -en	subordinator
Sie leiten einen Nebensatz ein.	They introduce a subordinate clause.
einleiten (er leitet ein)	to introduce, mark the start of

D 4

die Sonnenbrille, -n	sunglasses
der Regenschirm, -e	umbrella

D 5

der Wintermantel, ̈	winter coat

E 1

Reisen bildet.	Travel educates. *English idiom:* "Travel broadens the mind."
bilden	to educate, form, shape, train

die Zusammenfassung, -en	summary
Humboldt, Wilhelm von (1767–1835)	*Scholar and statesman. He was a friend of Goethe and Schiller.*
Sancho Pansa	*A character in Cervantes' most famous novel, 'Don Quixote'.*
der Eseltreiber	donkey-drover
Cervantes, Miguel de (1547–1616)	*Spanish writer*
Man muß Land und Leute kennen.	One must get to know the country and its people.
kennen*	to know (through learning), to get to know
Bedeuten die Ausdrücke links und rechts das gleiche oder das Gegenteil?	Do the phrases/expressions on the left and on the right mean the same or the opposite?
der Ausdruck, ⸚e	expression, phrase
der, das, die gleiche	the same
begreifen*	to grasp the meaning of
der Dichter, - (in f)	poet/writer
der Literat, -en	literary person
mit eigenen Augen sehen	to see with one's own eyes
unvollständig	incomplete
Don Quixote	*Main character in Cervantes' novel 'Don Quixote', this spelling being germanised from 'Quijote'.*
verständlich	intelligible, clear
schildern	to describe, portray, depict
die wahren literarischen Gestalten	the true literary forms
wahr	true
literarisch	literary
die Gestalt, -en	form
E 2 das Geburtshaus, ⸚er	the house where … was born

> Wer den Dichter will verstehen, muß in Dichters Lande gehen.
> Whoever wants to understand the poet must go into the poet's country.

Frankfurt am Main	Frankfurt-on-the-Main (River)

> **der Main** (river): *Rivers have an article:* der Rhein (Rhine), der Neckar, die Donau (Danube), die Elbe

	Großer Hirschgraben 23	*The address of the house where Goethe was born. One can look around it.*
	Goethestraße	*A street in Frankfurt, but not the one in which the house where Goethe was born is located.*
E 3	die Sprachferien *(Plural)*	holidays to learn a language
	der Ferienkurs, -e	holiday course
	die Gruppe, -n	group
	der Spaziergang, ⁼e	walk, going for a walk
	die Wanderung, -en	excursion, hike, walking tour
	der Ausflug, ⁼e	outing
	Rothenburg	Rothenburg *(See map inside back cover of textbook.)*
E 4	Marseille	Marseilles
	das Fahrrad, ⁼er	bicycle
	Nordafrika	North Africa
	die Abenteuerlust	the joy of adventure
	Athen	Athens
	Chicago	Chicago
	die Ferien *(Plural)*	holidays
	indisch	Indian
	Bogota	Bogota
	die Pilgergruppe, -n	group of pilgrims
	Rom	Rome
	beten	to pray
	jugoslawisch	Yugoslavian
	besuchen	to visit
	der Besuch, -e	visit
	die Bildungsreise, -n	study tour
	die Abenteuerreise, -n	adventure holiday
	die Pilgerreise, -n	pilgrimage
	die Geschäftsreise, -n	business trip
	die Besuchsreise, -n	visit, journey just to see a country
	Was gehört zusammen?	What belongs together?
	zusammengehören	to belong together
E 7	die Reisewerbung	travel advertisement
	Entwerfen Sie ein Werbeplakat!	Design an advertising placard.
	entwerfen* (du entwirfst, er entwirft)	to design, invent
	das Werbeplakat, -e	advertising placard
	der Werbeprospekt, -e	advertising prospectus
	deutschsprachig	German-speaking

F 1 das Königreich, -e

kingdom *(Negative words are used as names in this poem. That's why they are given initial capitals. Otherwise, of course, they would be written with small letters.)*

nirgendwo	nowhere
Schau mal!	Look!
Ach Quatsch!	Oh, rubbish!
der Quatsch	rubbish, nonsense
Die erste Strophe geht so. = Die erste Strophe heißt so.	The first verse goes like this . . ./says . . .
. . . liegt tief am Meeresgrund	. . . lies deep at the bottom of the sea
liegen* *(geographisch)*	to lie *(in a place)*
der Meeresgrund	the sea-bed
der Grund (Meer), -	bed *(of the sea)*
der König Sowieso (Herr/Frau Sowieso)	King Anyhow
der König, -e (in f)	king
sowieso	anyhow, in any case
niemand	nobody, no one
Die zweite Strophe steht da auch noch, oder?	The second verse is there too, isn't it?
schwierig	difficult
keinesfalls	in no case, on no account
Sie ist erstaunlich klein.	She is astonishingly small.
erstaunlich	astonishingly, amazingly
das Tier, -e	animal
wie eine große weiße Ente	like a big white duck
die Ente, -n	duck
ein langer Hals	a long neck
der Hals, ⸚e	neck
lang	long
der Schwan, ⸚e	swan
der Schwanenhals, ⸚e	swan's neck
Sie sagt beständig: Nein!	She says continually: No!
Das klingt auch auf deutsch wie ein Gedicht.	In German that also sounds like a poem.
klingen*	to sound

Danke für das Kompliment.	Thank you for the compliment. *(In Germany people are always happy to receive a compliment, and they say thank you for it.)*
das Kompliment, -e	compliment
Ich habe frei übersetzt.	I have translated it freely.
frei übersetzen	to translate freely.
Wort für Wort übersetzen	to translate word for word.
abschreiben* (ich schreibe ab)	to copy
F 2 die Negation, -en	negation
jemand	someone
irgendwo	somewhere
auf jeden Fall	in any case
der Fall, ⁼e	case
nirgends	nowhere
regieren	to rule, govern

8

AS

Man muß die Feste feiern, wie sie fallen.	Make hay while the sun shines.
Erzähl mir keine Märchen!	Don't tell me stories!
Erst die Arbeit, dann das Vergnügen!	Business before pleasure.

erst (= zuerst) first (at first)

der Rattenfänger von Hameln the Rat-catcher of Hameln.
The English title is: The Pied Piper of Hamelin.
(Local legend: A rat-catcher is supposed to clear the town of Hameln of rats. When the citizens of the town don't want to give him the reward they promised, he abducts all the children of the town.)

lebendig living

romantisch romantic

Alemannische Fastnacht Alemannic Carnival *(In the South German region: The day or night before the beginning of Lent (the period of fasting before Easter). Still today the* Fastnacht *is celebrated with processions and traditional masks.*

Rheinischer Karneval Carnival of the Rhineland *(The* Fastnacht *in the Rhineland is called* Karneval.)

A 1 die Landeskunde study of national customs

interviewen to interview

Teils – teils. partly, in part

Die Arbeitsleistung ist zwar ständig gestiegen, aber . . . The work-performance has indeed risen constantly, but . . .

die Arbeitsleistung, -en work-performance, work-achievement

zwar . . ., aber indeed/it is true . . . but

ständig constant(ly); permanent(ly)

Die Arbeitszeit ist immer mehr zurückgegangen. The hours of work are being reduced more and more.

die Arbeitszeit, -en the working hours, hours of work

immer mehr	more and more
zurück gehen* (sie geht zurück)	to go back, to recede; go down, fall
der Achtstunden tag, -e	8-hour day
die 40-Stunden-Woche, -n	40-hour week
In einigen Bereichen arbeitet man schon weniger als 40 Stunden.	In a few areas they already work less than 40 hours.
der Bereich, -e	area, field; scope, range
weniger als	less than
Die Gewerkschaften fordern sogar noch weitere Arbeitszeit-verkürzungen.	The trade unions are actually demanding even shorter working hours.
die Gewerkschaft, -en	trade unions

Die Gewerkschaften

The trade unions in the German Federal Republic organize themselves according to industrial alliances. The individual trade unions are amalgamated into the German Trade Union Alliance (Deutscher Gewerkschaftsbund = DGB). *The main aims are: full employment, workers' social security, and worker participation.*

---

fordern	to ask, demand; to claim, require
die Arbeitszeit verkürzung, -en	reduction in working hours
Und wie sieht es mit dem Urlaub aus?	And what about holidays?
aus sehen* mit *(unpersönlich)*	to look *(impersonal: as a passive)*
Der beträgt heute durchschnittlich sechs Wochen.	Today it comes to an average of six weeks.
betragen* *(i. d. Bed. nur 3. Person Sg. und Pl.)*	to come to, amount to
durchschnittlich	average
Dazu kommen noch die gesetzlichen Feiertage.	In addition to that there are the public holidays.
gesetzlich	statutory, according to the law, legal
der Feier tag, -e	*day that is a public holiday*
Davon haben wir mehr als andere Länder.	We have more of those than other countries.
mehr als	more than
Im internationalen Vergleich arbeiten wir weniger als andere.	An international comparison shows that we work less than others.

der Vergleich, -e		comparison

Vergleiche	weniger als	less than
	mehr als	more than
	so viel wie	as much as

seit einiger Zeit	for some time
seit	for *(a period of time);* since *(a point in time)*
die Einstellung, -en	*here:* attitude; adjustment, setting, engagement
sich verändern	to change
der einzige Sinn des Lebens	the only purpose in life
der, das, die einzige	only
der Sinn	purpose, meaning, interest
das Leben	life
Bei uns war das schon immer so.	It has always been like that with us.
schon immer	always (schon = already, *included in the present perfect verb form in English.)*
Man kann das aber auch ganz anders sehen.	But one can see it quite differently.
etwas anders sehen*	to see something differently/in another way
Und wann kommt die 35-Stunden-Woche?	And when is the 35-hour week coming?
A 2 freie Zeit	spare time, leisure
die Verkürzung, -en	shortening, reduction
die Wochenstunde, -n	hours per week
tarifliche Wochenarbeitszeit	weekly working hours in the wages agreement *(Weekly working hours which have been written into the wage agreement negotiated by the trade unions with the employers.)*
die Wochenarbeitszeit	weekly working hours
der Urlaubstag, -e	day's leave
der Jahresurlaub	annual leave
die Jahres-Sollarbeitszeit, -en	annual working hours
die Industrie, Industrien	industry
Schweden	Sweden
die Arbeitswoche, -n	the working week

der Industrie‿arbeiter, - (in f)	industrial worker
Immer mehr Bundesbürger halten die Freizeitgestaltung für wichtiger.	More and more citizens think that leisure activities are more important.
der Bundesbürger, - (in f)	Federal citizen
halten* für (du hältst für, er hält für)	to look upon, consider, think, take to be
die Freizeit‿gestaltung	leisure activities
38,5-Stunden-Woche für Metallarbeiter!	38.5-hour-week for metal workers!
der Metall‿arbeiter, - (in f)	metal worker
A 3 die Erklärung, -en	explanation
die Graphik, -en	graphic arts; *here:* headlines in graphics
früher	earlier, formerly
A 5 Halten Sie bitte einen kleinen Vortrag über . . .	Please give a short lecture on . . .
einen Vortrag halten	to give a lecture
der Antwort‿satz, ⁼e	sentence giving the answer
B 1 der Tages‿ablauf, ⁼e	daily routine
das Kino, -s	cinema
anschließend	afterwards
die Diskothek, -en	discotheque
so um zwei	at about two
Ich war so müde.	I was so tired.
müde	tired
Ich bin fast im Stehen eingeschlafen.	I almost fell asleep standing up.
ein‿schlafen* (du schläfst ein, er schläft ein)	to go to sleep, fall asleep
Wie der Arbeitstag verlaufen ist?	How the day at work turned out?
der Arbeits‿tag, -e	working day, day at work
verlaufen* *(i. d. Bed. nur 3. Person Sg. und Pl.:* Der Arbeitstag verläuft normal.)	to pass, proceed, take its course, turn out
pünktlich	punctually
das Geschäft, -e	business, firm
Sonst ist nichts Besonderes passiert.	Nothing special happened during the rest of the time.
sonst	otherwise, besides, at other times
passieren *(nur 3. Person)*	to pass, come to pass, take place
Na, nix. (nix = nichts)	No, nothing.

8

auf̯wachen (ich wache auf)	to wake up (I wake up)
Das geht Sie nichts an!	That's nothing to do with you!/That's none of your business!
an̯gehen*	*here:* to concern, to have to do with; to approach; to apply
der Park, -s	park
rauchen	to smoke
das Bier, -e	beer
trinken*	to drink
nach dem Aufstehen	after getting up
auf̯stehen* (du stehst auf, er steht auf)	to get up (out of bed)
laufen* (du läufst, er läuft)	to run
der Früh̯sport	early morning sport/exercise
sich treffen* mit (ich treffe mich mit . . .)	to meet (someone)
treffen* (du triffst, er trifft)	to meet
mieten	to rent, hire
Bremen	Bremen *(See map inside back cover of textbook.)*
der Kunden̯besuch, -e	visiting a client
Wir haben zusammen Mittag gegessen.	We had lunch together.
der Mittag, -e	midday
das Büro, -s	office
diktieren	to dictate
Wollen Sie das im Detail wissen?	Do you want to know that in detail?
das Detail, -s	detail
die Freizeit	spare time
direkter Fragesatz	direct interrogative sentence (question)
der Frage̯satz, ⁼e	interrogative sentence, question
indirekter Fragesatz	indirect interrogative sentence, question
B 3 nach̯fragen (ich frage nach)	to enquire *(in the context: simply repeating the question)*
die Nach̯frage, -n	the enquiry
Zeit gewinnen für die Antwort	to gain time to think up an answer
B 4 die Perfekt̯form, -en	the form of the perfect tense
die Orts̯veränderung, -en	change of place
die Zustands̯veränderung, -en	change of condition
reflexive Verben	reflexive verbs

B 7	der Witz, -e	joke
	der/die Angestellte, -n	employee
	der Chef, -s	boss
	zweimal	twice
	Notieren Sie bitte!	Please note.
	minus	minus
C 1	das Heimatˌmuseum	local museum (museum of local history, etc)
	das Museum, Museen	museum
	der Saal, Säle	large room or hall (here: the display rooms)
	in vorhistorischer Zeit	in prehistoric time
	vorˌhistorisch	prehistoric
	historisch	historic
	das Wappen, -	coat-of-arms
	der Hahn, ¨e	cock
	krähen	to crow
	Kikeriki	The sound the cock makes. English equivalent: Cock-a-doodle-doo!
	Wir kennen die Anfänge nur aus einer Inschrift und aus Sagen.	We know the beginnings only from the inscription and from legends.
	die Inˌschrift, -en	inscription
	die Sage, -n	legend, saga, tradition
	der Stein, -e	stone, monument
	Im Jahre 4 × 13 befreite der Herr des Regenbogens die Stadt.	In the year 4 times 13 the Lord of the Rainbow freed the town. (The time reckoning in this text is fantasy.)
	befreien	to free
	Er besiegte den unsterblichen Drachen.	He conquered the immortal dragon.
	besiegen	to conquer, to defeat
	unsterblich	immortal

Das Gegenteil ausdrücken:

sterblich	mortal	**un**sterblich	immortal
höflich	polite	**un**höflich	impolite
interessant	interesting	**un**interessant	uninteresting

---

der Drache, -n	dragon
die Zeitˌrechnung, -en	chronology; reckoning of time; era
das Rätsel,-	puzzle, mystery

8

In den Sagen heißt es:	In the legend it says:
Es heißt, daß . . .. *(unpersönlich)*	It says that . . ..
im 7. Jahrhundert unserer Zeitrech-	In the 7th century according to our
nung	calendar
wahrscheinlich	probably
das Jahrhundert, -e	century
der Tyrann, -en	tyrant
das Volk, ¨er	the people

people	
1. Leute	all people
2. Volk	the people of a specific region (a nation)
3. Bevölkerung	inhabitants

	die Burg, -en	castle
	strafen	to punish
	rauben	to steal; to abduct, take away
	die Alten	the old people
	klagen	to mourn, lament
	weinen	to weep
	töten	to kill
C 2	**heraus͜suchen**	to look for something in . . ., to seek something out
C 3	**bilden**	to form
C 4	**konjugieren**	to conjugate
C 5	**faule Ausreden**	poor excuses
	faul	bad, lazy, poor
	die Ausrede, -n	excuse, evasion
D 1	**verzweifelt**	in despair, desperate
	ratlos	helpless, at a loss
	um Hilfe rufen	to call for help
	rufen*	to call
	die Hilfe, -n	help
	Sie versprachen dem Retter eine hohe Belohnung.	They promised the rescuer a large reward.
	versprechen* (du versprichst, er verspricht)	to promise
	der Retter, - (in f)	rescuer, saviour
	die Belohnung, -en	reward
	der Abenteurer, - (in f)	adventurer

steigen* — to climb

Aber sie stürzten ab und fanden den Tod. — But they fell and met their death.

ab∫stürzen — to plunge down, fall, crash down

der Tod — death

Schließlich kam ein Fremder. — At last a stranger came along.

schließlich — at last, finally

ein Fremder, eine Fremde, *Plural:* Fremde — a stranger; a foreigner

Man weiß leider nicht genau, was dann geschah. — Unfortunately it is not known exactly what happened then.

geschehen* *(nur 3. Person Sg. und Pl.:* geschieht, geschehen) — to happen, to take place

erscheinen* — to appear

verschwinden* — to disappear

Ach, und ihr habt deshalb . . .. — Ah, and that's why you have . . ..

Genau! — Exactly!

die Regenbogen∫brücke, -n — rainbow bridge

das Regenbogen∫fest, -e — rainbow festival

das Märchen, — fairy tale, legend

der Historiker, -(in f) — historian

eine vernünftige Erklärung — a rational explanation

vernünftig — rational, reasonable

D 2 Die meisten sind unregelmäßig. — Most of them are irregular.

die meisten — most (of them)

D 3 Was reimt sich? — What rhymes?

sich reimen *(nur 3. Person Sg. und Pl.)* — to rhyme

die Präteritum∫form, -en — past tense form

die Präsens∫form, -en — present tense form

D 4 der Herz∫infarkt, -e — heart attack

Zürich — Zürich

das Taxi, -s — taxi

ein Taxi nehmen — to take a taxi

D 5 Die Bestätigungs∫frage, -n — question of confirmation

die Bestätigung, -en — confirmation, verification

erwarten — to expect

das Märchen∫buch, ¨er — book of fairy tales

die Instituts∫bibliothek, -en — library of the institute

D 6 **bestätigen** — to establish, confirm, verify

D 7 die Heimat∫geschichte — local history

der Ort, -e — region

E 1 Das Märchen vom nächtlichen Regenbogen	The Legend of the Nocturnal Rainbow
nächtlich	nocturnal, nightly
arm	poor
der Bursche, -n	lad, fellow, youth
Er hatte keine Habe und keine Bleibe.	He had no possessions and no roof over his head.
die Habe	goods; possessions, property
die Bleibe	shelter, roof over his head
besitzen*	to own, possess
blind	blind
Die Sonne ging auf.	The sun came up.
auf‿gehen* *(i. d. Bed. nur 3. Person Sg.)*	*here:* to rise; to evaporate; to expand
die Stadt, ⸚e	town, city
prächtig	splendid, fine
weit und breit	far and wide
breit	wide
die Blume, -n	flower
welk	withered, faded, shrivelled
Selbst vom Himmel fielen die Regentropfen . . .	Even from Heaven raindrops fell . . .
selbst (= sogar)	even
die Träne, -n	tears
Warum tragt ihr Trauer?	Why are you in mourning?
Trauer tragen*	to be in mourning
der Jüngling, -e	young man
sterben* (du stirbst, er stirbt)	to die
Wie geht das zu?	How is that?/How did that come about?
alle unsere Kinder	all our children
der Neu‿mond	new moon
der Mond, -e	moon
wieder‿kommen* (er kommt wieder)	to come again, to return
verwüsten	to devastate, to lay waste
der Weg, -e	the way
die Rettung	rescue
um Mitternacht	at midnight
die Mitternacht	midnight

8

nimmer	never *(Made up from* nie mehr. *This poetic form is found mostly in folk songs and fairy tales.)*
Die Uhr schlug neun.	The clock struck nine.
schlagen* *(i. d. Bed. 3. Person Sg. und Pl.)*	to beat; *here:* to strike
die Turmₗuhr, -en	clock tower
Der Drache kam geflogen.	The dragon came flying.
Er flüsterte dem Hahn ganz leise Zauberworte ins Ohr.	He whispered magic words very softly in the cock's ear.
flüstern	to whisper
leise	quietly, softly
das Zauberₗwort, -e	magic word

```
            ↗ Pl.: Wörter = single, individual words
  das Wort
            ↘ Pl.: Worte = a saying, verdict, motto; declaration
```

das Ohr, -en	ear
so laut, daß	so loud that
so . . . daß	so . . . that
erwachen	to awake, to wake up
erleuchten	to light up
alsbald	forthwith, immediately *(poetic form for* bald)
zischen	*here:* to hiss; to speak in an undertone
fauchen	to hiss, spit
Es half ihm nichts.	It didn't help him at all.
helfen* + *Dativ* (du hilfst, er hilft)	to help
sich niederₗlegen (er legt sich nieder)	to lie down, to go to bed *(Poetic form for* sich hinlegen; *similar to the English 'fairy tale' form:* He laid himself down.
die Drachenₗburg, -en	Dragon fortress
zurückₗlaufen* (du läufst zurück, er läuft zurück)	to run back
leuchten	to light up, shine
Alle Menschen tanzten vor Freude.	All the people danced for joy.
die Freude	joy

87

die Heimat	home(land)
Und wenn sie nicht gestorben sind, so leben sie noch heute.	And if they have not died, they are still living like that today. (= And they all lived happily ever after.)

E 4

die Zeitform, -en	tense
Die Verbform, -en	the form of the verb
monologisch	in monologue
der Textteil, -e	part of the text

F 1

der Nationalfeiertag, -e	national holiday
die Theatervorstellung, -en	theatre presentation, performance
das Naturtheater,	open-air theatre
Es hat richtig geregnet.	It really rained!
richtig *(Adverb)*	really *(adverb)*; certainly
Du hast wirklich viel verpaßt.	You really missed a lot.
verpassen	to miss (an opportunity or a train, *etc.)*
echt	real, genuine
der Schauspieler, - (in f)	actor
der Zuschauer, - (in f)	spectator *(in the plural:* the audience)
die Nationalhymne, -n	the national anthem
Ihr müßt mal richtig der Reihe nach erzählen.	You must tell it in the right order/sequence.
der Reihe nach	according to the order

F 2

der Gebrauch	the use
Mir geht ein Licht auf.	Now I begin to see./Now the light's beginning to dawn.
das Licht, -er	light
beide	both
Was ist der Unterschied?	What is the difference?
Da mußt du die verschiedenen Texte ansehen.	You must look at the different texts.
ansehen* (du siehst an, er sieht an)	to look at, consider

F 4

korrekt	correct
untypisch	not typical, untypical

F 5

die Drachengeschichte, -n	story of the dragon
der Zauberspruch, ¨-e	incantation, charm, spell
achtgeben* (du gibst acht, er gibt acht)	to pay attention to
wachen	to be awake/on guard/keep watch
Es wird vollbracht.	It will be carried out.
vollbringen*	to accomplish, achieve, carry out

weich — gentle; soft; smooth

sogleich (= sofort) — immediately, straight away

das Sonnenlicht — sunlight

böse — bad, evil, wicked; angry

♪ **2** die Chemie — chemistry

♪ **3** Ojemine! — a sound of lament (*eg.* Woe is me!)

Ach und Weh — alas and woe (a *doleful outcry*)

wagen — to venture, risk

jagen — to hunt, pursue

aus der Bahn bringen — to throw . . . off balance

juchhe, juchhei, juchheirassa — *sounds of rejoicing, shouting with joy*

AS

Sei mir gegrüßt, mein Sauerkraut, holdselig sind deine Gerüche.	Greetings, my sauerkraut, Your smells are the loveliest.

der Geruch, ⸚e   smell, odour, fragrance

Es wird mit Recht ein guter Braten gerechnet zu den guten Taten.	It is right that a good roast does justice to good deeds.

der Braten, -   roast (of meat)
die Tat, -en   deed, action, act

Hunger ist der beste Koch. Essen und Trinken hält Leib und Seele zusammen.	Hunger is the best cook. Eating and drinking keep body and soul together.

der Hunger   hunger
der Leib, -er   body (Leib *is an obsolete word now only used as high style and poetic language.*)
die Seele, -n   soul
die chinesische Küche, die indische Küche, . . .   Chinese cooking, Indian cooking, . . .

A 1 **die Einladung, -en**   invitation
Wir feiern den Geburtstag unserer jüngsten Tochter. Wir möchten Sie herzlich dazu einladen.   We are celebrating the birthday of our youngest daughter, and you are most cordially invited to come to the party.

ein|laden* (du lädst ein, er lädt ein)   to invite
die Adresse, -n   address
mit herzlichen Grüßen   with warm greetings

herzlich	*from the heart, but not 'hearty'*

der Gruß, ⸚e   greeting
das Baby, -s   baby
Dürfen auch die beiden Kinder mitkommen?   May the two children also come with us?

dürfen* (ich darf, er darf)	to be permitted, may
Soll ich meinen dunklen Anzug anziehen?	Shall I put on my dark suit?
sollen* (ich soll, er soll)	to be obliged to, have to, must
formell	formal
Ich bleibe aber in Jeans!	But I'm staying in jeans!
die Jeans *(Plural)*	jeans
Das erlaube ich nicht!	I won't allow that!
erlauben	to allow
Laß sie doch, Hans!	Leave her alone, Hans!
lassen* (du läßt, er läßt)	to leave, to let be
verbieten*	to forbid
Na, wie üblich.	Oh, as usual.
üblich	usual, customary, in common use
die Schokolade	chocolate
Oder lieber eine Flasche Wein?	Or a bottle of wine instead?
die Flasche, -n	bottle
der Wein, -e	wine
der Alkohol	alcohol
Mir ist alles ziemlich unklar.	It's all a little vague/unclear to me.
unklar (≠ klar).	not clear, vague, obscure
etwas (= ein bißchen)	a little
Müssen wir vorher im Restaurant essen?	Do we have to eat beforehand in a restaurant?
vorher	beforehand, in advance, before
das Restaurant, -s	restaurant
essen* (du ißt, er ißt)	to eat
beachten	to consider, to pay heed to
noch einmal	once again
an̦rufen* (ich rufe an)	to call, to ring up, telephone
unhöflich (≠ höflich)	impolite
A 3 das Verbot, -e	prohibition
fremder Wunsch/Wille	assumed wish (assuming someone else wishes it)
der Auftrag, ̈e	order, charge; commission
A 4 die Diskussion, -en	discussion
A 5 die Feier, -n	celebration
die Verhaltenșregel, -n	rule of conduct
B 1 Wie geht es Ihnen?	How are you?
das Essen	food
das Besteck, -e	cutlery/knife, fork and spoon

9

Am besten schmeckt mir hier das Gemüse.	What I like best here are the vegetables.
schmecken (nur 3. Person Sg. und Pl.)	to taste
das Gemüse	vegetable
gießen* (du gießt, er gießt)	to water (plants); to pour, sprinkle
Nochmals vielen Dank!	Thank you once again
Die Reise ist ein großes Erlebnis.	The trip is a great experience.
das Erlebnis, -se	experience
ausgezeichnet	excellent
das Rezept, -e	recipe
Das Essen schmeckt besser als zu Hause.	The food tastes better than at home.
nach unserer Rückkehr	after our return
die Rückkehr	return (from a place)
Herzlichst Ihre . . .	Affectionally/cordially yours . . .
Touristik International	International Tourism

> Johannisstrasse = Johannisstraße
> *The style of writing* ss *for* ß *is found in some artistic scripts and computer writing. If you write a word with* ß *in capitals you put* SS, *eg.* GROSSMUTTER. *In the German-speaking area of Switzerland the style of writing* ss *in place of* ß *is officially permitted.*

Hier spielt Zeit keine Rolle.	Here time is of no importance.
eine Rolle spielen	to play a part
die Rolle, -n	part, role
neulich	recently
Pünktlich um 18 Uhr waren wir da – wie es sich gehört.	We were there punctually at 6 p. m. – as is proper.
sich gehören (unpersönlich: Das gehört sich/gehört sich nicht.)	to belong to the occasion (Impersonal: That's right, seemly./That isn't the way to behave.)
Langsam verliere ich hier das Zeitgefühl.	I'm slowly losing a feeling for time.
verlieren*	to lose
das Zeitgefühl	the feeling for time
das Gefühl, ¨e	feeling
auf die Uhr gucken	to look at the clock, to keep one's eye on the clock
gucken	to look, glance at

hoffen	to hope
Hintere Ledergasse	*street name meaning literally* 'rear Leather Lane'
die Gasse, -n	lane, alley
Hoffentlich geht es Dir gut.	I hope you are well.

> **Du, Dich, Dir** *etc have initial capitals in letters.*

hoffentlich	hopefully
Das Essen war ganz große Klasse!	The food was really high class!
große Klasse sein	to be high class
der Reis	rice
die Sorte, -n	kind, sort
toll	great! terrific!
Tschüß!	Bye-bye.
Bis bald!	See you soon.
bald	soon
B 2 **der Freund, -e** (in f)	friend
B 3 **die Hauptmahlzeit, -en**	main meal
das Frühstück	breakfast
das Brot, -e	bread
das Brötchen, -	bread roll
die Butter	butter
die Margarine	margarine
die Marmelade, -n	jam
das Ei, -er	egg
der Käse	cheese
die Wurst, ¨e	sausage
das Müsli, -s	muesli
die Corn-flakes *(Plural)*	cornflakes
das Getränk, -e	drink, beverage
der Kaffee	coffee

> *Note:*
> **das Café, -s** *place you go for snacks etc.*
> **der Kaffee** *drink*
> *The German word* Kaffee *has almost the same pronunciation as the word 'cafe' as used in English. So do not confuse the drink with the place you go for snacks, etc.*

der Tee	tea
die Milch	milk
der Kakao	cocoa
warm	warm, hot
die Suppe, -n	soup
die Kartoffel, -n	potato
die Nudel, -n	noodle
die Erbse, -n	pea
die Bohne, -n	bean
der Kohl	cabbage
der Salat, -e	salad; lettuce
das Fleisch	meat
der Schweine‿braten, -	roast pork
der Rinder‿braten, -	roast beef
der Kalbs‿braten, -	roast veal
der Braten, -	the roast
die Soße, -n	sauce, gravy
das Schnitzel, -	steak, cutlet
der Fisch, -e	fish
gekocht (gekochter Fisch)	boiled (boiled fish)
kochen	to cook, boil, stew
gebraten (gebratener Fisch)	fried (fried fish)
braten* (du brätst, er brät)	to fry; roast
der Nachtisch	dessert
das Obst	fruit
der Apfel, ¨	apple
die Birne, -n	pear
die Banane, -n	banana
das Eis	ice cream
der Pudding, -e	pudding *(of the custard type, like blancmange)*
das Abend‿essen, -	evening meal
der Schinken, -	ham
das Mineral‿wasser	mineral water
der Saft, ¨e	fruit juice
Ich vermisse ein Glas Wasser.	I miss a glass of water. (I am used to one.)
vermissen (ich vermisse, du vermißt, er vermißt)	to miss
das Glas, ¨er	glass
das Stäbchen, -	*here:* chopsticks
das Messer, -	knife

die Gabel, -n	fork
Wir essen aus Schüsseln und nicht von Tellern.	We eat from bowls and not from plates.
die Schüssel, -n	bowl
der Teller, -	plate
das Sauerkraut	Sauerkraut *is pickled white cabbage.*
Das ist wohl ein Vorurteil.	That's really a prejudice.

B 4

die Geschmacksfrage, -n	question of taste
Nicht besonders.	Not particularly.
besonders	particularly, especially
die Zunge, -n	tongue

B 5

der Käsekuchen, -	cheesecake
Beethoven, Ludwig van (1770–1827)	*German composer*
Nein, überhaupt nicht.	No, not at all.

B 6

die Kongruenz, -en	congruity, agreement
der Numerus, Numeri	number *(in grammar)*
das Subjekt, -e	subject
Subjekt und Verb stimmen in Person und Numerus überein.	Subject and verb agree in person and number.
übereinstimmen	to agree, to be in accord

B 7

ausländisch	foreign
Der Anteil aller ausländischen Restaurants an allen Gaststätten betrug 34 %.	Foreign restaurants constituted 34 % of all the public eating houses.
der Anteil, -e	share, part, constituent
die Gaststätte, -n	restaurant, public eating place

Bezeichnungen für Nationalität

Sprache	**Adjektiv**
Sie spricht **G**riechisch.	ein **g**riechisches Restaurant
Sie spricht **I**talienisch.	ein **i**talienisches Restaurant
Sie spricht **P**ortugiesisch.	ein **p**ortugiesisches Restaurant

(In German the name of the language is written with an initial capital, and (unlike English) the adjective with a small letter.)

C 1

der Kuchen, -	cake
backen	to bake
die Küche, -n	kitchen
der Vanillezucker	vanilla sugar

9

der Zucker	sugar
der Vanillegeschmack	taste of vanilla
die Vanille-Essenz, -en	vanilla essence
Feiner Nußkuchen	Fine nutcake *(tasty or delicately flavoured)*
fein	fine, delicate, refined
der Nußkuchen, -	nutcake
die Zutat, -en	ingredients
g = das Gramm	gram
das Salz, -e	salt
etwas geriebene Zitronenschale	some grated lemon peel *(If you want to try out the recipe make sure that you use a lemon that has not been sprayed with fertilizer.)*
reiben*	to grate, scrape
die Nuß, Nüsse	nut, nuts
das Mehl	flour
das Päckchen, -	little packet
das Backpulver	baking powder
die Waage, -n	scales
der Meßbecher, -	measuring cup/jug
messen* (du mißt, er mißt)	to measure
die Tasse, -n	cup
der Löffel, -	spoon
die Umrechnungstabelle, -n	conversion table
Die Butter schaumig rühren.	Stir the butter until it is creamy.
schaumig	creamy, frothy
rühren	to stir
Nach und nach den Zucker dazugeben.	Add the sugar little by little.
nach und nach	little by little, gradually
dazugeben* (du gibst dazu, er gibt dazu)	to add
das Gewürz, -e	spice, condiment, seasoning
das Eigelb	egg yolk
mischen	to mix
unterrühren (Rühren Sie die Nüsse unter!)	to stir into/through (Stir the nuts into the mixture).
der Teig, -e	dough, paste
fest	firm
Das Eiweiß steif schlagen und unterheben.	Beat the egg white stiff and fold in.

das Eiweiß	egg white
steif	stiff
schlagen* (du schlägst, er schlägt)	to beat
unter͜heben* (Heben Sie das Eiweiß unter!)	to fold; *literally:* to lift from underneath. (Fold in the egg white.)
die Gugelhupf-Form, -en	a cake form/mould *(from an Austrian dialect)*
ein͜fetten (Fetten Sie die Form ein!)	to grease, oil (Grease the mould.)
ein͜füllen (Füllen Sie den Teig ein!)	to fill in (Pour in the cake mixture.)
circa	about
200 °C	*(In Germany the degrees of temperature are measured in Celsius.)*
= **200 Grad Celsius**	
der Grad, -e	degree
Celsius (1701 – 1744)	*Swedish astronomer; the division of the scale of temperature into 100 degrees between freezing point and boiling point was named after him.*

°C	°F (Fahrenheit)
100	212
90	194
80	176
70	138
60	140
50	122
40	104
30	86
20	68
10	50
0	32

Kuchen stürzen und mit Puderzucker bestäuben.	Turn the cake upside down and dust with icing sugar.
stürzen	to overturn; to upset; *here:* to turn over (upside down)
der Puder͜zucker	icing sugar
bestäuben	to dust, to strew
Sie gab noch etwas Rum dazu.	She added a little rum to it.
der Rum	rum
das Schokoladen͜stückchen, -	flaked chocolate, chocolate chips
lecker	delicious, tasty
Bloß keinen Alkohol!	Only no alcohol!
Sonst komme ich in Teufels Küche!	Otherwise I'll be in a real mess!
sonst	otherwise, or
der Teufel, -	the devil
probieren	to try

der Bauch schmerz, -en	stomach-ache
der Bauch, ⸚e	stomach
der Schmerz, -en	pain, ache
C 2 der Eß löffel, - (EL)	tablespoon
der Kaffee löffel, -	teaspoon
um rechnen (Rechnen Sie bitte um!)	to convert (into); (Please convert into . . .)
Was wiegt wieviel?	What weighs what (how much)?
wiegen*	to weigh
die Kaffee tasse, -n	coffee cup
ml = der Milliliter, -	millilitre
die Flüssigkeit, -en	liquid
der Liter, -	litre
das Fett, -e	(cooking) fat
das Öl, -e	oil
der Pulver kaffee	instant coffee
kg = das Kilogramm, -	kilogram
C 3 **auf schreiben*** (ich schreibe auf)	to write down
zuletzt	last, finally
aus probieren (ich probiere aus)	to test, try out
Rosinen im Kopf haben	to plan great things, be full of crazy ideas, be full of oneself *(The poem makes a pun with the turn-of-phrase:* Rosinen im Kopf haben, *and* Rosinen (raisins) *which are baked in a cake.)*
die Rosine, -n	raisin
C 4 der Kinder arzt, ⸚e (Kinderärztin f)	children's doctor, pediatrician
die Zeitschrift, -en	magazine
planen	to plan
Improvisieren ist für sie verdächtig, ja fast unmoralisch.	Improvisation is suspicious or even immoral for them.
improvisieren	to improvise
verdächtig	suspicious
unmoralisch	immoral
Sie konnte nicht „aus der Hand arbeiten".	She couldn't work intuitively (without any help).
Sonst wissen sie nicht weiter.	Otherwise they don't know what to do next.
weiter wissen* (ich weiß weiter, er weiß weiter)	to know what to do next

beweglich sein	to be active, versatile
anpassungsfähig	adaptable
der Asiate, -n (Asiatin f)	Asian
das Stichwort, ⸚er	*here:* caption

D 1

Kaffee-Kantate	Coffee Cantata
Ei, wie schmeckt der Kaffee süsse,	Ay, how sweet the coffee tastes,
lieblicher als tausend Küsse,	lovelier than a thousand kisses,
milder als Muscaten-Wein.	milder than wine from the muscatel.
Kaffee, Kaffee muß ich haben,	Coffee, coffee I must have,
und wenn jemand mich will laben,	and if anyone wants to refresh me
ach, so schenkt mir Kaffee ein.	ah, then pour out coffee for me.

der Kuß, Küsse	kiss, kisses
die Poesie	poetry
Bach, Johann Sebastian (1685–1750)	*German composer*
komponieren	to compose

Lob des Kaffees	In Praise of Coffee
Kaffee, Kaffee ist mein Leben,	Coffee, coffee is my life,
Kaffee ist ein Göttertrank.	Coffee is a drink of the gods
Ohne Kaffee bin ich krank.	Without coffee I am ill.
Selbst der süße Saft der Reben	Even the sweet juice of the grapes
muß Kaffee den Vorzug geben.	Must bow to coffee.

das Lob	praise
krank	ill
die Rebe, -n	grape, vine
im Durchschnitt	on average
der Durchschnitt, -e	the average
Schweitzer, Albert (1875–1965)	*missionary doctor in Africa*
D 2 das Wiener Kaffeehaus	*Vienna Coffee House*
der Gast, ⸚e	guest
die Bildungsstätte, -n	place of education/formation
die Orientierung, -en	orientation
Zweig, Stefan (1881–1942)	*Austrian writer*
um 1940	about 1940

die Auto‿biographie, -n	autobiography
die Jahrhundert‿wende, -n	turn of the century
künstlerisch	artistic
der Zusammenhang, ⸚e	connection, association
Sie waren intellektuell beweglich und international orientiert.	They were intellectually active and internationally oriented.
intellektuell	intellectual(ly)
(sich) orientieren	to orient(ate) (oneself)

D 3

beim Kaffeetrinken	(engaged in) drinking coffee
Also, ehrlich . . .	Now, honestly . . .
der Milch‿kaffee	coffee with milk
die Strafe, -n	punishment
Über Geschmack soll man nicht streiten.	One should not quarrel about taste.
der Geschmack	taste
streiten* über (du streitest)	to argue, quarrel about
Ich bin sicher, daß . . .	I am sure/certain that . . .
der Frühstücks‿kaffee	breakfast coffee
schwach	weak
der Espresso, -s	espresso coffee
Puh!	*a noise of surprise and rejection*
Der ist ja stärker als stark.	That is certainly stronger than strong.
die Hölle	hell
die Sahne	cream
Irish Coffee	Irish Coffee
die Spezialität, -en	specialty
Irland	Ireland
irisch	Irish
bestehen* aus	to consist of
der Whiskey, -s	whisky
empfehlen* (du empfiehlst, er empfiehlt)	to recommend
Türkischer Kaffee	Turkish Coffee
Der riecht gut!	That smells good!
riechen*	to smell
Igitt!	How nasty/disgusting!
der Kaffeesatz	coffee grounds
die Art, -en	kind
ironisch	ironic
Er zieht Herrn Klinger ein bißchen durch den Kakao.	He makes Herr Klinger look a little ridiculous.

jemanden durch den Kakao ziehen*	to make someone look ridiculous
D 5 die Komparation	comparison
der Positiv, Positivformen	positive (forms)
der Komparativ, -e	comparative
der Superlativ, -e	superlative
am meisten	the most
an̦geben* (du gibst an, er gibt an)	*here:* to pretend, boast
der Angeber, - (in f)	someone pretentious, a boaster
D 8 häßlich	ugly
sicher	sure, certain
klug	clever
reich	rich
schlecht	bad

Vergleiche

etwas weniger . . . als	a little less . . . than
nicht so . . . wie	not so . . . as
nicht ganz so . . .wie	not quite so . . . as
fast so . . . wie	almost as . . . as
wie	as
genauso . . . wie	just as . . . as

D 9 das Teehaus, ̈er	tea house
„Zum grünen Blatt"	"To/At the Green Leaf"
das Blatt, ̈er	leaf, blade *(of grass);* petal; sheet *(of newspaper)*
♪ **1 die Maschine, -n**	machine
der Anfangșbuchstabe, -n	letters at the beginning *(of words)*
der End̦buchstabe, -n	letters at the end
das Kabel, -	cable
der Schlag, ̈e	blow, knock, bang
platt	flat, level
♪ **2 das Picknick**	picnic
die Pampelmuse, -n	grapefruit
purzeln	to tumble, somersault
plötzlich	suddenly
die Pappel, -n	poplar
der Popo, -s *(Abk.* Po)	bottom *(of a person), (the 'behind')*
das Hallo	a to-do, a hullabaloo
die Platte, -n	plate *(of meats, etc)*
Pappelhusen	*Words made up for the nonsense poem.*
Pampelmusen̦gebabbel	

10

AS	Brücken schlagen	to build bridges, form connections with others
	eine goldene Brücke bauen	to build a golden bridge - a bridge of reconciliation
	die Esels‚brücke	mnemonic, memory aid
	Halten Sie das Bild an die Nase!	Hold the picture up to your nose.
	die Nase, -n	nose
A 1	der Fach‚sprachen‚kurs, -e	specialist language course
	die Fach‚sprache, -n	technical language
	der Intensiv‚kurs, -e	intensive course
	das Semester, -	semester
	die Voraussetzung, -en	prerequisite, what is presumed *(eg. knowledge before taking a course)*
	die Berufstätigkeit	employment in a (particular) job
	die Tätigkeit, -en	*here:* occupation; profession; activity, function
	technisch	technical
	das Fach, ⁻er	subject, branch, specialty
	Sie können sich mit Kollegen über technische Grundfragen unterhalten.	You can talk to colleagues about basic technical questions.
	sich unterhalten* über (du unterhältst dich, er unterhält sich)	to talk/have a conversation about
	die Grund‚frage, -n	basic question/problem
	die Umgangs‚sprache	colloquial speech
	der Physiker, - (in f)	physicist
	gründliche Kenntnisse	sound/well-founded knowledge
	gründlich	thorough, well-based, sound
	die Kenntnis, -se	knowledge
	die Physik	physics, physical science
	die Struktur, -en	structure
	physikalisch	physical
	der Fach‚text, -e	scientific/specialist text
	erkennen*	to recognise
	Texte mit Hilfe eines Wörterbuches durcharbeiten	to work through texts with the aid of a dictionary
	Der Kurs wird nicht auf deutsch gehalten.	The course will not be held in German.
	Zur Zeit gibt es weder Fachsprachenkurse für Mediziner noch für Hotelangestellte.	At the moment there are neither courses for the medical profession nor for hotel employees.

10

zur Zeit	at the moment, at present
weder . . . noch	neither . . . nor . . .
der Mediziner, - (in f)	medical student or doctor
der/die Hotelangestellte, -n	hotel employee
Wir empfehlen den Besuch der allgemeinen Deutschkurse.	We recommend attending the general course in German.
allgemein	general
der Deutschkurs, -e	German course

A 2 Die Teilnehmer sind alle Spezialisten. — The participants are all specialists.

der Teilnehmer, - (in f)	participant
der Spezialist, -en (in f)	specialist
der Wissenschaftler, - (in f)	*Person engaged in research in an academic field, not necessarily one of the exact sciences.*
der Professor, -en (in f)	professor
mindestens	at least
der Doktorand, -en (in f)	candidate for a Doctorate
sich langweilen (ich langweile mich)	to become bored (I am bored)
der Inhalt, -e	content(s)
sinnvoll	*here:* useful; sensible
der Grundkurs, -e	basic course
danach	after that
der Rat, Ratschläge	advice

A 3

die Kursberatung, -en	advice on courses
die Variation, -en	variation
Bitte, um was geht's denn?	Yes, what is it?/What can I do for you?
gehen* um (*unpersönlich:* es geht um . . .)	to have to do with, be about
der/die Bekannte, -n	acquaintance
fertig	finished
der Lesekurs, -e	reading course

Danke

Danke.	Herzlichen Dank
Vielen Dank.	Besten Dank.
Tausend Dank.	Danke schön.
Vielen Dank für die Auskunft.	Ich danke Ihnen für die Einladung.

10

A 4	die Verneinung, -en	negative
	der Chemiker, - (in f)	chemist *(in chemistry)*
B 1	die Relativitätstheorie, -n	Theory of Relativity
	die Theorie, -n	theory
	Einstein, Albert (1879–1955)	*physicist; discoverer of the Theory of Relativity*
	die Radierung, -en	etching
	Liebermann, Max (1847–1935)	*painter and graphic artist*
	spazieren‿gehen* (ich gehe spazieren)	to go for a walk
	heiß	hot
	die Schwanen‿feder, -n	swan's feather
	die Feder, -n	feather
	der Vogel, ¨	bird
	biegen*	to bend, curve
	die Geduld verlieren*	to lose patience
	die Geduld	patience
	der Arm, -e	arm
	strecken	to stretch
	gerade (≠ gebogen)	straight (≠ bent)
	beugen	to bend, flex
	der/die Blinde, -n	blind man/woman
	der Erklärungs‿schritt, -e	step in the explanation
B 2	**die Blindheit**	blindness
	flüssig	liquid, flowing
	ähnlich	similar
	die Ähnlichkeit, -en	similarity
	möglich	possible
	die Süßigkeit, -en	sweetness; *pl* sweets
	Wie praktisch!	How practical/useful!
B 3	der Ober‿begriff, -e	heading, group, classification
	die Hitze	heat
B 4	das Rätsel‿spiel, -e	riddle, puzzle
	raten* (du rätst, er rät)	to guess
	das Rätsel‿wort, ¨er	*the word you are trying to guess*
	der/die Verwandte, -n	relation (a *person*)
C 1	der Sprach‿unterricht	language lesson
	flüssig sprechen	to speak fluently
	korrekt sprechen	to speak correctly
	Ich finde, daß Sie uns nicht genug korrigieren.	I don't think you correct us enough.
	genug	enough

korrigieren	to correct
der Fehler, -	mistake
Das kommt darauf an.	That depends.
an|kommen* auf *(unpersönlich)*	to depend on
die Grammatik|übung, -en	grammar exercise
frei sprechen	to speak freely
vermeiden* (du vermeidest, er vermeidet	to avoid
die Umschreibung, -en	paraphrase
Im übrigen sind Fehler normal.	Anyway mistakes are normal.
im übrigen	in other respects; *here:* anyway
ohne Angst vor Fehlern sprechen	to speak without fear of making mistakes

C 2

die Aussage, -n	statement
Ich rede einfach drauflos.	I simply talk away.
drauflos|reden	to start talking, talk away *(i.e. without hesitating to think)*
Die Fehler interessieren mich nicht.	The mistakes don't interest me.
interessieren	to interest
zufrieden	quite happy
mit|reden (du redest mit, er redet mit)	to join in the conversation, talk with
schüchtern	shy, timid
mutig	courageous
zu Wort kommen*	to get (a chance) to speak
Mir fehlen die Wörter.	I'm speechless.
fehlen	to be missing/wanting, to be absent
Ich kann in Ruhe nachdenken.	I can think it over in peace.
nach|denken* (ich denke nach)	to think over, reflect on
Es stört mich, wenn	It disturbs me if/when . . .
stören	to disturb
Ich mache mir Notizen.	I take notes.
die Notiz, -en	note
sich Notizen machen	to make/take notes
die Rollen|karte, -n	card with the roles *(of the people on the list)*

C 3

der Fallschirm, -e	parachute
ab|springen* (ich springe ab)	to leap off/down
die Tiefe, -n	depth(s)
schweben	to soar, hover, float in the air

D 1

die Leseratte, -n	bookworm ("reading rat")

das Satzglied, -er	part of a sentence
die Ergänzung, -en	complement, completion
die Angabe, -n	statement
Hoppla!	Mind out!/Steady on!
die Lese͜brille, -n	reading glasses
Wozu?	For what purpose?/Why?
Womit?	By what means? *(What does she use?)*
D 2 Guten Appetit!	*It is said at the beginning of a meal; similar to American:* Enjoy your meal!
der Appetit	appetite
unglücklich	unhappy
E 1 die Satz͜verknüpfung, -en	sentence connector
Das Satzglied auf Position I stellt die inhaltliche Verknüpfung zwischen den Sätzen her.	The part of the sentence in Position I refers to the previous clause and connects it to the next one.
her͜stellen	to constitute, make, produce
inhaltlich	with regard to the contents
die Verknüpfung, -en	connector, connection
E 2 bestimmen	to decide, determine, ascertain
F 1 die Sprachlosigkeit	being without the use of language or speech
der Einwanderer, (Einwanderin f)	immigrant
berichten über (du berichtest, er berichtet)	to report on
die Kurz͜information, -en	brief information
die Realität, -en	reality
Überprüfen Sie Ihre Lösung!	Check your solution.
überprüfen	to examine, test; *here:* to check
die Politik	politics
ein͜kaufen (ich kaufe ein)	to buy, to go shopping
das Klein͜kind, -er	little child
der Mit͜schüler, - (in f)	fellow student
fest͜stellen (ich stelle fest)	to establish, confirm
der Streik, -s	strike
die Inflation, -en	inflation
„Das ist Käse."	"That's cheese". *This is also a play on words with the phrase* "Das ist Käse" *meaning* "That's all rubbish".
doppeldeutig	ambiguous, having two meanings
Das ist Unsinn.	That's nonsense.

der Unsinn	nonsense
F 2 Wirf mir den Ball zurück, Mitura!	Throw the ball back to me, Mitura.
zurück‿werfen* (du wirfst, er wirft)	to throw back
der Ball, ⸚e	ball
das Feld, -er	field, meadow
fangen* (du fängst, er fängt)	to catch

„pie-uka" (= Ball)	*Sound reproduction of*
„djuuta" (= gelb)	*Polish words in German*
„pschyjazjel (= Freund)	*writing.*
„bole" (= Ball)	*Sound reproduction of*
„kaha" (= gelb)	*Singalese words in German*
„mitura" (= Freund)	*writing.*

F 3

Deutsch lernen – ein Vergnügen!

Bau dir eine Brücke aus Wörtern	Build yourself a bridge of words
von Chicago bis München –	from Chicago to Munich -
jeder Satz	each sentence
macht einen neuen Schritt.	forms a new step.
Die deutsche Sprache	The German language
ist weit auszudehnen,	stretches out,
führt hoch hinauf ins Blaue,	leads high up into the blue,
zeigt dir kristallene Paläste	shows you crystal palaces
über den Wolken,	above the clouds,
schneidet Bogen,	cuts out arches,
doch fest verankert	but the pillars are firmly
stehen die Pfeiler.	anchored.
Komm mir zu Fuß entgegen	Come to me on foot
über den Ozean.	over the ocean.

bauen	to build
der Schritt, -e	step
der Fuß, ⸚e	foot
sprach-barriere = Sprachbarriere	language barrier
Schmerzt es dich eigentlich, wenn	Does it really give you pain when . . .
schmerzen *(i. d. Bed. unpersönlich:*	to give pain (It hurts.)
Es schmerzt mich.)	
Illustrieren Sie bitte die Gedichte!	Please illustrate the poems.
♪ 2 die Phonetik	phonetics

AS	die Universität, -en	University
	Trier	Trier
	die Wohnungsˌvermittlung	accommodation arrangements
	das Gästeˌhaus, Gästehäuser	guest house
	Unterbringung am Sprachinstitut	provision of accommodation in the language institute
	die Kosten *(Plural)*	cost
	die Kaution, -en	deposit, security
	der Mietˌvertrag, ⸚e	lease
	die Hausˌordnung, -en	rules of the house
	die Begegnung, -en	meeting, reception
	die Schlaflosigkeit	sleeplessness
	bemalen	to paint over, to colour
	irgend jemand	anybody, somebody
	das Stipendium, Stipendien	grant, scholarship
	der Deutschlandˌaufenthalt, -e	stay/period in Germany
A 1	Deutscher Akademischer Aus- tauschdienst e. V.	German service for academic exchange e.V. = *a registered Union/Association*
	die Stipendienˌzusage, -n	pledge/promise of a grant or scholarship
	der Stipendiat, -en (in f)	the holder of the grant/scholarship
	das Heimatland, ⸚er	home country
	die Zusage, -n	pledge, promise
	Hast du denn schon alle Papiere zusammen?	Have you got all the papers you need?
	die Papiere *(Plural)*	papers
	das Flugˌticket, -s	flight ticket
	das Ticket, -s	ticket
	der Reiseˌpaß, Reisepässe	passport
	der Impfpaß, Impfpässe	vaccination certificate
	das Zeugnis, -se	certificate(s) *(of education, etc.)*
	Na klar!	Of course!
	Ach, ich bin schon ganz aufgeregt.	Oh, I'm already very excited.
	ach	*Ach! is a common exclamation.*
	aufgeregt sein	to be excited, stirred up
	Wer weiß, ob alles klappt.	Who knows if everything will be all right.
	ob	if, whether
	klappen *(i. d. Bed. unpersönlich: es klappt)*	to work out well, to be all right, *slang:* to come off

Göttingen	Göttingen *(See map inside back cover of textbook.)*
ein Taxi nehmen	to take a taxi
Bloß nicht!	Certainly not!
Das kostet ja ein Vermögen!	That will cost a fortune!
das Vermögen, -	fortune, wealth
die Entfernung, -en	distance (away)
Das gilt vielleicht für Lilaland.	Perhaps that's so for Lilaland.
gelten* für (*i. d. Bed. unpersönlich:* es gilt)	to be valid for, to hold good for
Alli fährt am besten mit dem Zug.	It's best for Alli to go by train.
der Zug, ⁻e	train
mit̪nehmen* (du nimmst mit, er nimmt mit)	to take with (you)
das Abend̪kleid, -er	evening dress
auf keinen Fall	not at all, never *(slang:* No way!)
Das kannst du viel zu selten anziehen.	You'd very seldom have the occasion to wear it.
selten	seldom
der Tip, -s	tip, hint
Ich frage mich, ob ich im deutschen Alltag überhaupt zurechtkomme.	I wonder whether I will get along at all with the daily life in Germany.
zurecht̪kommen* (ich komme zurecht)	to get along well with, succeed, manage
sicherlich	certainly, for sure
Ich habe Zweifel, ob meine Deutschkenntnisse ausreichen.	I am not sure whether my knowledge of German is sufficient.
der Zweifel, -	doubt
aus̪reichen (sie reichen aus)	to suffice, to be sufficient; to last
der Einkauf, ⁻e	the shopping
Ach, das schaffst du schon.	Oh, you will manage all right.
schaffen	to manage to do, to accomplish
die Schwierigkeit, -en	difficulty
die Verständigung	understanding
Die gehen schnell vorüber.	That will soon pass.
vorüber̪gehen*	to pass by/over/away
Ich wünsche dir jedenfalls eine gute Reise.	In any case I wish you a good trip.
wünschen	to wish
jedenfalls	in any case, by all means, however
Und schreib mir mal!	And write to me!

A 3 **der Ratschlag, ¨e**	advice, counsel, suggestions
das Vorwort, -e	preamble; preface, foreword
die Anreise	arrival
Eröffnung eines Bankkontos	opening of a bank account
die Bank, -en	bank
das Konto, Konten	account
die Wohnung, -en	flat, house, accommodation
die Post	post office
die Bundesˌbahn	railways (federal)
der Bus, -se	bus
die Straßenˌbahn, -en	tram, streetcar
die Kunst des Einkaufens	the art of buying
die Kunst	art, skill, dexterity
ärztliche Behandlung	medical treatment
ärztlich	medical
die Behandlung, -en	treatment
dabei haben	to have by or with you
die Ausweisˌpapiere *(Plural)*	identification papers
der Führerschein, -e	driving licence
das Paßˌfoto, -s	passport photo
nach Möglichkeit	where possible
die Möglichkeit, -en	possibility
eventuell	possibly, perhaps, if necessary
der Sprachˌführer, -	phrase book, elementary guide to the language
zur Not	if necessary
die Not, ¨e	necessity, need
das Tageˌbuch, ¨er	diary
A 5 das Ferienkursˌstipendium, -stipendien	grant for a holiday course
A 6 Lies' = Liese	*a short form of the name* Elisabeth
Oberammergau/Unterammergau	Upper- and Lower-parts of the district on the Amm River. Oberammergau *is famous for its Passion Play. (See map inside back cover of textbook.)*
gewiß	certain, sure
A 7 die Haarˌfarbe, -n	colour of hair
B 1 todˌmüde	dead tired
frieren*	to freeze, to be freezing
Das Zimmer wirkt schrecklich ungemütlich.	The room looks terribly uncomfortable.

wirken	*here:* to produce/give an impression *or* feeling
ungemütlich	uncomfortable
das Möbel, -	furniture
kaum	scarcely, hardly
der Koffer, -	suitcase
auf‚machen (ich mache auf)	to open (up)
das Bett, -en	bed
dünn	thin
die Decke, -n	cover, quilt, blanket

Note: **die Decke**
1. ceiling
2. cover, quilt, blanket

Plötzlich fühle ich mich sehr allein.	Suddenly I feel very much alone.
(sich) fühlen	to feel
Jetzt merke ich erst, wie sehr ich an meiner Heimat hänge.	Now I realize for the first time how attached I am to my homeland.
merken	to note, to see *(as to note)*
hängen* an	to be attached to, to be dependent on
sich fragen	to ask oneself
unbedingt	unquestioning, unconditional
Alles ist so kalt hier.	Everything here is so cold.
das Heimweh	home-sickness
der Zimmer‚nachbar, -n (in f)	neighbour in the next room
der Bett‚bezug, ⁻e	bed linen

---

*Alli Alga fortunately found a warm bedcover in the cupboard, probably a so-called **Federbett**, a linen bag filled with down feathers. For many Germans it is the same as for Alli Alga when they travel abroad; they are used to the warm feather bed, and find a thin woollen blanket which, they feel, doesn't encase the body in a soft, supple way.*

---

beziehen*	*here:* to cover, to stretch over
legen	to lay
stellen	to place
rücken	to move
kitschig	showy, trashy
das Blumen‚bild, -er	picture of flowers

das Regenbogenplakat, -e	rainbow chart/poster
hängen	to hang up, cause to hang, suspend

---

hängen - hängen an

Er hängte das Plakat an die Wand.
He hung the poster on the wall.

Er hing sehr an seiner Heimat.
He was very attached to his homeland.

---

sich setzen	to sit down
die Stimmung, -en	mood
Ich fühle mich viel wohler.	I feel much better.
sich wohlfühlen	to feel well
B 2 **verwechseln**	to confuse, to mix up
B 3 die Kugel, -n	sphere, globe, ball
die Pyramide, -n	pyramid
der Würfel, -	cube
C 1 die Wohnkultur	taste in/style of home décor
stolz	proud
Die „eigenen vier Wände" spielen im Alltagsleben eine immer größere Rolle.	One's "own four walls" play an ever greater role in daily life.

"Die eigenen vier Wände" *is more the equivalent of* "My home is my castle".

---

das Alltagsleben	the daily life, the routine
der Wohnstil, -e	style of living
die Wohnungseinrichtung, -en	furnishings in the house, flat, *etc*
beliebt	favourite
das Gesprächsthema, Gesprächsthemen	topic (of conversation)
der Prospekt, -e	prospectus
das Möbelhaus, Möbelhäuser	furniture store
dies (= das)	this, that
deutlich	clear
beeinflussen (du beeinflußt, er beeinflußt)	to influence
die Vorstellung, -en	idea, concept

der Leser, - (in f)	reader
der Kunde, -n (Kundin f)	customer
wecken	to waken, to arouse
der Wohngeschmack	taste in furnishings *etc.*
jahrelang	for many years, year-long
modern	modern
klare Linien	clear, plain or distinct lines
klar	clear, pure, distinct, *etc*
die Linie, -n	line
der Schnickschnack	paraphernalia
Alte Möbel . . . galten als „un-modern".	Old furniture was considered old-fashioned.
das Ornament, -e	ornament
rund	round
gelten* als (du giltst, er gilt)	to pass for, to be considered as
unmodern	old-fashioned
wieder	again
teuer	expensive
die Alternative, -n	alternative
die Funktion, -en	function
das Arbeitszimmer, -	work-room, study
◦ 2 Weimar	Weimar *(See map inside back cover of textbook.)*
Rechts davor steht ein Papierkorb.	In front of it on the right there is a wastepaper basket.
davor	in front of it
der Papierkorb, ⸚e	wastepaper basket
um den Tisch herum	around the table
um . . . herum	around
die Kommode, -n	chest of drawers
die Stirnwand, ⸚e	front or facing wall
dazwischen	between them
der Spiegel, -	mirror
das Schreibpult, -e	writing desk
darauf	on it
die Figur, -en	figure
das Pronominaladverb, Pronominaladverbien	pronominal adverb
daneben	next to
◦ 3 klassisch	classical
das Möbelstück, -e	piece of furniture
der Werbetext, -e	advertising text

die Regalkombination, -en — combination bookcase
das Regal, -e — bookshelf

> Werther Wilhelm Meister Egmont
> Faust Gretchen Mephisto Tasso
> Erlkönig Lotte
>
> *Names of people in the novels and plays of Goethe.*

D 1

das Schülerzimmer, - — schoolgirl's/-boy's room
unordentlich — disorderly, untidy
individuell — individual, personal
das Wohnzimmer, - — living-room
das Nomadenzelt, -e — nomad's tent
unter freiem Himmel — in the open air
die „Gute Stube" — drawing room, parlour
die Stube, -n — room
voll — full
gemütlich — comfortable, cosy
das Lehrerehepaar, -e — *married couple who are teachers*
das Ehepaar, -e — married couple
modisch — stylish, fashionable

> modisch — *corresponding to the fashion*
> modern — *up-to-date*

organisiert — organised
funktional — functional
das Schloß, Schlösser — castle
beeindruckend — impressive
alleinstehend — single, living alone
der Ingenieur, -e (in f) — engineer
sachlich — to the point, essentially practical
nüchtern — sensible, moderate
repräsentativ — representative
die Rangskala, Rangskalen — scale of rank

D 2 Wo würden Sie sich am wohlsten fühlen? — Where would you feel most at home?
das Zelt, -e — tent
das Metall, -e — metal
das Glas — glass
die Sachlichkeit — functionality

der Stil, -e	style
schick	elegant, with good taste *(Adopted into the German way of writing; sometimes one also finds it written chic.)*
Ich fühle mich dort wohl, wo Ordnung herrscht.	I feel happy where order prevails.
die Ordnung	order, tidiness
herrschen	to prevail; to be in control
Gemütlich ist es dort, wo alles herumliegen kann.	It is comfortable where everything can lie around.
herum‿liegen*	to lie around; to surround
So bekommt das Zimmer eine persönliche Note.	The room then has a personality/ personal note.
die Note	note, mark
schwer (≠ leicht)	heavy (≠ light)

---

schwer ≠ leicht

1. difficult ≠ easy

   Deutsch lernen ist nicht <u>schwer</u>. Es ist <u>leicht</u>.

   Learning German is not <u>difficult</u>. It is <u>easy</u>.

2. heavy ≠ light

   Du hast so große, <u>schwere</u> Möbel. Mir gefallen <u>leichte</u> Möbel besser.

   You have such big, <u>heavy</u> furniture. I like <u>light</u> furniture better.

---

die Bequemlichkeit	comfort
bequem	comfortable
das Sofa, -s	sofa
eng (≠ weit)	narrow (≠ wide)
leer (≠ voll)	empty (≠ full)
3 der Konjunktiv, -e	subjunctive
tun*	to do
4 **begründen**	to give reasons for
die Wahl, -en	choice
Genau wie ich.	Exactly like me!
Warum gefällt dir denn gerade Raum B?	Why exactly do you like Room B?
gerade *(Partikel)*	exactly, just
5 mehrmals	several times
die Hausfrau, -en	housewife
der Lehrling, -e	apprentice

der Firmen‿chef, -s (in f)	head of a firm
D 8 zusammengesetzte Substantive	substantive built up of more than one noun
der Schlüssel, -	key
der Schranktür‿schlüssel, -	key of the cupboard door
das Grund‿wort, ¨er	basic word
der Schreib‿tisch, -e	desk
♪ 1 sich voll‿füllen	to fill oneself up
♪ 2 der Kontext, -e	context
die Vor‿information, -en	initial/previous information
♪ 5 **bereit**	ready, prepared
beraten* (du berätst, er berät)	to advise
brechen* (du brichst, er bricht)	to break
der Bericht, -e	report
♪ 6 **teil‿nehmen*** (du nimmst teil, er nimmt teil)	to take part

AS

> Land- und Forstwirtschaft = Landwirtschaft und Forstwirtschaft
> *In German the base word* (Wirtschaft = economy) *need not be repeated,
> but can in the first instance be replaced by a stroke to indicate its
> omission.*

die Außenˌwirtschaft	foreign trade
die Entwicklungsˌpolitik	policy with regard to developing countries

A 1

die Landwirtschaftsˌmesse, -n	agricultural show/fair
die landwirtschaftliche Nutzfläche	area under agricultural cultivation
der Betrieb, -e	business; *here:* farm or agricultural unit
die Durchschnittsˌgröße, -n	average size
Mio = Millionen	millions
ha = Hektar = 10 000 m²	a hectare = 10,000 square metres
der/die Berufstätige, -n	working person
berufstätig	working, in work
der Vertreter, - (in f)	representative
die Landwirtschaft	agriculture
Worum geht es?	What is it?
Ach, darüber wundern Sie sich!	Oh, that surprises you!
sich wundern über + *Akk.*	to be surprised at/about
Sie denken sicher bei Deutschland nur an die Industrie, nicht wahr?	You only think of industry when you think of Germany, don't you?
denken* an + *Akk.*	to think of
nicht wahr ?	*The question-tag at the end of a statement which varies in English:* -, aren't they? -, won't you? -, do you? etc.
sprechen* von + *Dat.*	to speak about
sich interessieren für + *Akk.*	to be interested in
informieren über + *Akk.*	to inform about, to tell something about
Kann die Bundesrepublik sich selbst versorgen?	Can the Federal Republic provide for itself?
sich versorgen	to provide for/maintain one-/itself
der Bauer, -n (Bäuerin f)	farmer
subventioniert (*Infinitiv:* subventionieren)	subsidized
das Produkt, -e	product

12

sich spezialisieren auf + *Akk.*	to specialize in
einführen (sie führen Obst ein)	to import
das Bio-Gemüse	bio-vegetables
die Lebensmittel *(Plural)*	foodstuffs
vergiften	to poison
der Kunstdünger, -	artificial manure, fertilizer
die Chemikalie, -n	chemicals
produzieren	to produce
Das klingt doch gut.	That sounds good.
klingen*	to ring; *here:* to sound
Man hat die Verwendung von Chemikalien streng genug geregelt.	The use of chemicals has been regulated strictly enough.
die Verwendung, -en	use
streng	strong, strict
regeln	to regulate
die Untersuchung, -en	test
das Landwirtschaftsministerium, -ministerien	Ministry of Agriculture
das Bio-Produkt, -e	bio-product

> The prefix **Bio** and the adjective **biologisch** are today synonymous with "healthy" in connection with foodstuffs.

Ach wirklich?	Oh, really?
sich entscheiden* für + *Akk.* (du entscheidest dich, er entscheidet sich)	to decide for/in favour of
Worüber wundern sich Koto K. und Nuri N.?	What are Koto K. and Nuri N. surprised about/at?
der Bioladen, ⁻	Bio-shop
der Laden, ⁻	shop
das Getreide	cereals, corn, grain
die Feige, -n	fig
ungespritzt (≠ gespritzt)	unsprayed
die Orange, -n	orange
umweltfreundlich	not damaging to the environment
die Umwelt	environment
Wasch- und Reinigungsmittel, -	detergents and cleansers
das Waschmittel, -	detergent
freilaufende Hühner	free-range hens

das Huhn, ¨er	hen

> *Modern egg-production businesses keep thousands of hens in large numbers of cages.* **Freilaufende Hühner** *are, on the other hand, those with sufficient space in the hen-run and can scratch in the sand. They are thought to lay better eggs because "they are happier". In Bio-shops the only eggs sold are those from free-range hens.*

	unbehandelte Milch	untreated milk
3	der Messebesucher, - (in f)	visitor to the fair
	wissen* von + *Dat.*	to know about
	fragen nach + *Dat.*	to ask about
	antworten auf + *Akk.*	to answer
4	**die Bedeutung, -en**	meaning
	verknüpfen	to join
	die Präpositionalergänzung, -en	prepositional complement
	der Kasus, -	case *(in grammar)*
	die Akkusativpräposition, -en	prepositions followed by the accusative
	gegen	against, opposite
	die Dativpräposition, -en	prepositions followed by the dative
	die Wechselpräposition, -en	prepositions after which the case may change
	fidibum	*A word made from children's rhymes. The rhyme may help to keep the rule in your head.*
	immerzu = immer	always
6	**die Sache, -n**	thing
7	präzisieren	to make precise, to define
	beginnen* mit + *Dat.*	to begin with
	bitten* um + *Akk.*	to ask about
	lachen über + *Akk.*	to laugh about
	erzählen von + *Dat.*	to tell of
	aufhören mit + *Dat.*	to stop
1	das Kommunikationsproblem, -e	problem of communication
	die Wirtschaftsverhandlung, -en	economic negotiations
	der Geschäftspartner, - (in f)	business partner
	der Partner, - (in f)	partner
	die Verhandlung, -en	negotiation
	die Geschäftsleute *(Plural)*	business people

Düsseldorf	Düsseldorf *(See map inside back cover of textbook.)*
verkaufen	to sell
die Industrie͜anlage, -n	industrial plant/installations
ab͜reisen (ich reise ab)	to depart, to go away
Wir konnten uns sein Verhalten nicht erklären.	We couldn't understand his behaviour.
das Verhalten	behaviour, conduct
sich etwas erklären	to explain something
irgendwas = irgendetwas	anything at all
ab͜fahren* (du fährst ab, er fährt ab)	to depart
erfreuen	to be happy about, to be pleased
ungeduldig	impatient(ly)
Darauf konnten wir nicht antworten.	We couldn't answer that.
Herr Schneider wollte Ihnen sein Projekt vorstellen.	Mr Schneider wanted to present his project to us.
jemandem etwas vorstellen	to present/introduce something to someone

B 4 Gack Gack Gaaack!

The sound a hen makes, from: gackern = to cackle

C 1

der Lohn, ⸚e	wage(s)
das Gehalt, ⸚er	salary
aktuell	current, of the present
besorgen	to procure, see to, attend to
der Monats͜verdienst, -e	monthly earnings
der Verdienst, -e	earnings
brutto	gross
Stand: April 1983	state *or* condition in April 1983
der Briefträger, - (in f)	postman
der Arbeiter, - (in f)	worker
der/die Bank͜angestellte, -n	bank clerk/employee
der Richter, - (in f)	judge
der/die leitende Angestellte	executive

der leitende	Angestellte	ein	leitender Angestellter
die leitende	Angestellte	eine	leitende Angestellte
Plural:			
die leitenden	Angestellten		leitende Angestellte

Davon gehen noch durchschnittlich 33 % ab.	From that an average of 33 % is deducted.
abˌgehen* von + *Dat.*	to go/come off
die Steuer, -n	tax
die Sozialˌabgabe, -n	social security payment/tax
netto	nett
C 2 der Preis, -e	price
ein Paar Schuhe	a pair of shoes

ein **P**aar Schuhe	a pair of shoes
ein **P**aar Strümpfe	a pair of stockings
ein **p**aar Fragen	a few questions
ein **p**aar Kinder	a few children

Notice that when the two things belong together (shoes), the word for pair Paar *has a capital letter in German.*
"ein Paar" also means a married couple, or two people who belong together.

C 3 das Presse- und Informationsamt der Bundesregierung	The Press and Information Office of the Federal Government
die Regierung, -en	the government
Welckerstr. = Welckerstraße	Welcker Street *(The abbreviation -str. for* Straße *is connected to the name of the street.)*
geehrt	honoured
Sehr geehrte Damen und Herren, . . .	*This is the formal way of addressing people in a letter, equivalent of "Dear Sir,"*

In German one now always uses in formal letters:
Sehr geehrte Damen und Herren,

Vielen Dank im voraus.	Many thanks in advance/in anticipation
im voraus	in advance, anticipation
C 4 das Bundesministerium für Ernährung, Landwirtschaft und Forsten	Federal Ministry of Food, Agriculture and Forests
das Bundesministerium für wirtschaftliche Zusammenarbeit	Federal Ministry for Economic Co-operation
die Entwicklungsˌpolitik	policy with regard to developing countries

	das Bundesministerium für Arbeit und Sozialordnung	Federal Ministry of Labour and Welfare
	der Bundesverband der Deutschen Industrie (BDI)	Federal Union of German Industry
	Deutscher Gewerkschaftsbund (DGB)	German Trade Union Congress
D 1	**der Supermarkt, ⁝e**	supermarket
	die Qualität	quality
	preiswert	good value
	ABC-Supermarkt	ABC Supermarket
	der Kopfsalat, -e	lettuce
	das Stück, -e	piece, item
	belgisch	Belgian
	die Markenbutter	brand (trade mark) butter
	die Marke, -n	sign, token, brand
	Pfd. = das Pfund	pound weight (lb)
	die Olive, -n	olive
	dänisch	Danish
	das Hähnchen, -	chicken
	bulgarisch	Bulgarian
	die Tomate, -n	tomato
	das Rindfleisch	beef
	die Vollmilch	full-cream milk
	mexikanisch	Mexican
	der Honig	honey
	Neuseeland	New Zealand
	die Kiwi, -s	kiwi fruit
	das Landbrot, -e	farm-baked/country bread
	der Schweizer Käse	Swiss cheese
	tatsächlich	actually
	der Pfennig, -e	one-hundredth of a Mark
	die Mark, -	*the Mark is the German currency*
D 2	der Relativsatz, ⁝e	relative clause
	das Relativpronomen, -	relative pronoun
	die Nationalität, -en	nationality
	Bulgarien	Bulgaria
	neuseeländisch	from New Zealand
	luxemburgisch	from Luxembourg
	britisch	British
D 4	Mexiko	Mexico
D 5	die Europäische Gemeinschaft (EG)	the European Community
	europäisch	European

die Gemeinschaft, -en	community
Formen Sie die Sätze bitte um!	Please transform the sentences.
um͜formen	to transform, reshape
der Franzose, -n (Französin f)	Frenchman/-woman
der Brite, -n (Britin f)	Briton
der Däne, -n (Dänin f)	Dane
der Belgier, - (in f)	Belgian
der Ire, -n (Irin f)	Irishman/-woman
der Luxemburger, - (in f)	man/woman from Luxembourg
E 1 die Öl͜nuß, Ölnüsse	oil nut, nut that yields oil
Jumbo	Jumbo (*A name often given to elephants in children's books.*)
Chelonia	*a name*
das Entwicklungs͜land, ⸚er	developing country
das Reis͜feld, -er	rice field
die Ölnuß͜maschine, -n	oil-nut machine
Von wegen!	How do you make that out!
hungern	to go hungry, to be hungry
Warum hat man denn nicht einfach die Reisfelder behalten?	Why did they not simply keep the rice fields?
behalten* (du behältst, er behält)	to retain, to keep
Wegen der Ölnüsse, logisch!	Because of the oil-nuts, obviously.
wegen + *Gen.*	because of
logisch	logical, clear
an͜bauen (sie bauen . . . an)	to cultivate
das Milch͜pulver	milk-powder
bezahlen	to pay for
auf einmal	for once
lecker	tasty, delicious
E 2 **weiter͜denken*** (ich denke weiter)	to think further/some more
das Industrie͜land, ⸚er	industrial country
vernichten	to destroy
E 3 landwirtschaftliche Produkte	agricultural products
die Kategorie, -n	category
der Tabak	tobacco
der Weizen	wheat, corn
der Maniok, -s	manioc, cassava
die Baumwolle	cotton
E 4 das Industrie͜produkt, -e	industrial product
die Hacke, -n	hoe
die Schaufel, -n	shovel

	der Traktor, -en	tractor
	der Pflug, ⸚e	plough
	die Zugkuh, ⸚e	yoked cow or ox
	der Mähdrescher, -	combine-harvester
E 5	**das Plakat, -e**	poster, placard
	die Wirtschaftspolitik	economic policy
E 6	Teufelskreis der Armut	vicious circle of poverty
	der Teufel, -	devil
	der Kreis, -e	circle
	die Armut	poverty
	gering	low, little
	die Produktivität	productivity
	mangelhaft	deficient, incomplete
	die Ausbildung, -en	education, instruction, training
	die Produktion, -en	production
	die Krankheit, -en	illness
	das Wachstum	growth
	die Nahrung	nourishment, nutrition
	der Konsum	consumption
	die Ersparnis, -se	saving
	die Investition, -en	investment
	das Nord-Süd-Problem, -e	the north-south problem
	Wenig Nahrung ist ein Grund für Krankheit.	Little nourishment is a reason for illness.
	ein Grund sein für + *Akk.*	to be a reason for
	Krankheit führt zu geringer Leistung.	Illness leads to low achievement.
	führen zu + *Dat.*	to lead to
	die Leistung, -en	achievement
♪ 1	erweiterte Nominalgruppe	extended/expanded nominal group
	die Sprechmelodie	intonation
	das Kissen, -	cushion, pillow
♪ 3	Fritz	Fritz
	fischen	to fish
♪ 4	der Ingenieur, -e (in f)	engineer

AS Internationale Filmfestspiele Berlin · International Film Festival Berlin
die Festspiele *(Plural)* · festival

A 1

> Hier bin ich Mensch, hier darf ich's sein!
> Here I am a human being, here I may be so!
>
> *An often-used quotation from Goethe's drama "Torquato Tasso". It*
> *expresses one's feelings of well-being in a place.*

sich beschäftigen mit + *Dat.* · to occupy oneself with
die Freizeit‚aktivität, -en · leisure activity
Beide Gruppen – und zwar 65 Prozent der leitenden Angestellten und 56 Prozent der Arbeiter – · Both groups – namely 65 % of the executives and 56 % of the workers –
und zwar · namely, in fact, that is
Darunter kann ich mir nichts Genaues vorstellen. · I can't imagine exactly what that means.
sich etwas vorstellen (können) · to (be able to) imagine something

> **vorstellen**
>
> Darf ich mich vorstellen? Mein Name ist . . .
> May I introduce myself? My name is . . .
>
> Darf ich Ihnen Frau Bauer vorstellen?
> May I introduce Mrs Bauer (to you)?
>
> Herr Schneider wollte sein Projekt vorstellen.
> Mr Schneider wanted to present his project.
>
> Darunter kann ich mir nichts vorstellen.
> I can't imagine what that is/means.

Das Fernsehen spielt dabei eine wichtige Rolle. · Television plays an important role there.
das Fernsehen · television
eher · rather
die „Freizeitpassivität" · "leisure passivity"
Spazierengehen steht an dritter Stelle. · Going for a walk takes third place.
die Stelle, -n · place
der Zweck, -e · purpose, goal
seltsam · peculiar, odd

125

13

umhergehen* (ich gehe umher)	to stroll about
im Freien	in the open air
zur Erholung	for relaxation
die Erholung	recuperation, relaxation
Sport treiben*	to take part in sport
allerdings	to be sure, of course
befragen	to question
aktiv	active
etwa (= circa)	about, approximately
16 beziehungsweise 18 Prozent	16 and 18 per cent respectively
das heißt	that is, . . .

---

heißen

Wie heißen Sie? – Mein Name ist . . .
What is your name? – My name is . . .

Wie heißt das auf deutsch?
What is that in German?

In alten Sagen heißt es: . . .
In the old legends it says: . . .

„Gemütlich" zu Hause bleiben – was heißt das?
To stay "gemütlich" at home – what does that mean?

---

die Sportveranstaltung -en	sporting event
wegfahren* (du fährst weg, er fährt weg)	to go away/out
verreisen	to go on a journey
der Garten, ⸚	garden
Basteln	handicrafts
Handarbeiten	manual work
aufräumen (ich räume auf)	to tidy up, to put in order
reparieren	to repair
sich ausruhen (ich ruhe mich aus)	to rest (I am taking a rest.)
Schach spielen	to play chess
das Schach	chess
der Mitmensch, -en	fellow human being
der Verein, -e	club, association
mitarbeiten (ich arbeite mit)	to work with
dazuverdienen (ich verdiene dazu)	to earn in addition

sich weiterbilden (ich bilde mich weiter)	to educate oneself further (I am doing further study, *etc.*)
die Ausstellung, -en	exhibition
musizieren	to make music
die Partei, -en	political party
B 1 Silvia	Sylvia
der Taxifahrer, (in f)	taxi driver
der Fahrer, - (in f)	driver
das Privattheater, -	private theatre
das Staatstheater, -	state theatre
das Steuergeld, -er	tax money
der Zuschuß, Zuschüsse	extra allowance, subsidy
der Staat, -en	the state
unterstützen	to support, assist, prop up
Da wird die Kunst abhängig und geht kaputt.	In that way art becomes dependent and is ruined.
die Kunst	art
abhängig sein	to be dependent
kaputtgehen	to go to ruin, to be broken down or lost
die Unterstützung, -en	support, assistance
Das meiste wird von den Schauspielern selbst gemacht.	Most things are done by the actors themselves.
das meiste	most things
das Bühnenbild, -er	stage set
der Kartenverkauf	ticket sales
das Ballett, -e	ballet
B 2 die Theateranzeige, -n	theatre notice, announcement of events at the theatre
das Theaterstück, -e	play, drama
B 3 das Aktiv	active voice *(grammar)*
die Passivform, -en	passive form
B 4 das Eßtheater	Eating Theatre/Theatre of Eating *(See the note on the "Begrüßungstheater" in Lesson 6, F4.)*
der Passivsatz, ⁼e	sentence in the passive
B 7 die Adjektivergänzung, -en	extension of the adjective
die Nominalergänzung, -en	extension of the noun
der Liebesfilm, -e	love film
das Paar, -e	couple, pair
ein Paar werden	to become a couple *(two people belonging together)*

127

13

B 8	das Kulturangebot, -e	cultural offering
	das Angebot, -e	offer
	„Journal am Morgen"	"News in the Morning" (*Programme on South German Radio about current topics, every morning from 8 to 8:15.*)
	das Stadttheater, -	municipal theatre
B 9	der Kulturaustausch	cultural exchange
	das Sprachgebiet, -e	language area
	das Gebiet, -e	area, region
	die Theatergruppe, -n	theatre group
	das Orchester, -	orchestra
	Brüssel	Brussels
♪ 1	die Verbalgruppe, -n	verb group
♪ 2	**verändern**	to change, alter
	die Veränderung, -en	alteration
♪ 3	die Kombination, -en	combination
	die Zeitungsnotiz, -en	newspaper item

zahm	tame
der Zaun	fence
der Züchter	breeder; cultivator
die Ziege	goat
der Zwerg	dwarf
verzweifelt	despairing
sich zwängen	to force oneself
zersplittert	broken up

In the text there are word-building games to practise the sound-combination [ts].

C 1	Karlstadt, Liesl (1892–1960)	*cabaret performer*
	Valentin, Karl (1882–1948)	*cabaret performer; These two often performed together.*
	die Unterrichtsstunde, -n	lesson
	der Reim, -e	rhyme
	die Mehrzahl, Mehrzahlformen	plural, plural forms
	bestehen* aus + *Dat.*	to consist of
	Jawohl.	Yes, indeed!
	die Mehlspeise, -n	pudding (*Austrian for sweets, cake*)
	Fremd ist der Fremde nur in der Fremde.	A foreigner is foreign only in a foreign country.

die Fremde	foreign country, abroad
Das ist nicht unrichtig.	That is not incorrect.
der Einheimische, -n	native of a country
der Münchner, - (in f)	person from Munich
Manchem Münchner ist das Hofbräuhaus nicht fremd.	To some people from Munich the Hofbräuhaus is not unknown.
mancher, manches, manche	some
das Deutsche Museum	The German Museum
das Museum, Museen	museum
die Vaterstadt, ⸚e	native town, home town
in mancher Hinsicht	in some respects
der Eisenbahnzug, ⸚e	railway train
durchfahren* (du fährst durch, er fährt durch)	to drive/pass through
Oho!	Oho!
der Kabarettist, -en (in f)	cabaret performer
der Komiker, - (in f)	comedian

C 3	das substantivierte Adjektiv	adjective made into a noun
C 4	das Sprachspiel, -e	language game
C 5	**die Prüfung, -en**	examination, test
	das Abstraktum, Abstrakta	*expressing an* abstract idea
D 1	Volleyball	volleyball
	fit	fit
	die Olympischen Spiele	the Olympic Games
	seitdem	since then
	So verbreitet wie Fußball ist diese Sportart natürlich noch nicht.	This sport is naturally not as widespread as football.
	verbreitet sein	to be widespread
	der Fußball (⸚e)	football
	die Sportart, -en	(type of) sport
	aggressiv	aggressive
	ab und zu	from time to time
	erstaunt sein über + *Akk.*	to be amazed at
	die Mannschaft, -en	team
	schreien*	shout, yell
	anfeuern (ich feure an)	to spur on
	begeistern	to inspire, to fill with enthusiasm
	die Spannung	tension
	der Kampf, ⸚e	fight, struggle
	die Höchstleistung, -en	best performance
	die Leistung, -en (*im Sport*)	performance (*in sport*)
	faszinierend	fascinating

13

halten* von (du hältst, er hält) + *Dat.*	to think of
der Wettbewerb, -e	contest
die Konkurrenz	competition, rivalry
gewinnen*	to win
der Krawall, -e	riot, violence
Das hat doch mit Sport nichts mehr zu tun.	That certainly no longer has anything to do with sport.
zu tun haben* mit + *Dat.*	to have to do with
der Ersatzkrieg, -e	substitute for war
ablehnen (ich lehne ab)	to reject
Man muß die positive Seite sehen.	One must see the positive side.
die Seite, -n	side
fördern	to advance, promote
die Völkerverständigung	understanding among peoples
geeignet sein	to be fitting, appropriate
Vorurteile abbauen	to break down prejudices
sich zusammensetzen (wir setzen uns zusammen)	to sit down together
das Freundschaftsspiel, -e	friendly game
ein Spiel/eine Reise organisieren	to organise a game/a trip
die Volleyballmannschaft, -en	volleyball team
das Tor, -e	goal
das Olympiastadion, -stadien	Olympic Stadium
D 2 das Fußballspiel, -e	football match
D 3 Er spielt, um fit zu bleiben.	He plays to keep fit.
D 5 **der Nationalismus**	nationalism
wildfremd	totally strange
ein wildfremder Mann	a total stranger
die U-Bahn, -en	underground train
das Dingsbums	what's-its-name, thingummy
die Olympiade, -n	Olympics
ankündigen (ich kündige an)	to proclaim, declare, advertise
die Jugend	youth
die Nation, -en	nation
der Sport-Bund	sports league
Eins zu null!	one – nil

130

14

AS Menschliches, Allzumenschliches

Human, All too Human
(The title of a philosophical work by Friedrich Nietzsche, 1844–1900)

A 1 mißverständlich — misleading
die Störung, -en — disturbance
Kommen Sie doch bitte rein! — Please come in.
reinkommen* = hereinkommen — to come in/inside
Mmh. — Mmh. *(In the text this sound indicates uncertainty.)*

Äh, es ist mir peinlich. — Ah, it is embarrassing for me.
peinlich — embarrassing, distressing; painful
Es fällt mir nicht leicht, darüber zu sprechen. — It is not easy for me to talk about it.
leichtfallen* *(unpersönlich: es fällt mir/dir/ihm leicht)* — to be easy *(for someone . . .)*
das Video-Band, ¨er — video tape
jemandem einen Gefallen tun* — to do someone a favour
der Gefallen, - — favour, kindness

---

jemandem einen Gefallen tun – jemanden um einen Gefallen bitten
to do someone a favour | to ask a favour of someone

Können Sie mir <u>einen Gefallen tun</u>?
Can you do me a favour?

<u>Diesen Gefallen tue</u> ich Ihnen gern.
I'll be pleased to do this favour for you.

Darf ich Sie <u>um einen Gefallen bitten</u>?
May I ask a favour of you?

Ich möchte die Bänder zurückhaben. — I would like to have the tapes back.
das Band, ¨er — tape
etwas zurückhaben* wollen — to want to have something back
leihen* — to lend
unmöglich — impossible
ungeschickt — inept, gauche
zurückhaltend — reserved
Sagen Sie dem Herrn doch einfach, daß es sich um ein Mißverständnis handelt. — Simply tell the man that there has been a misunderstanding.

14

sich handeln um + *Akk. (unpersönlich:* es handelt sich um . . .)	to be a point/question of (It's a question of)
Ist das bestimmt nicht zu unhöflich?	Is that really not too rude?
bestimmt (= sicher)	really, surely
theoretisch	theoretically
sich verhalten* (du verhältst dich, er verhält sich)	to behave, act, conduct oneself
über den eigenen Schatten springen*	to jump over one's own shadow *(i.e. to force oneself to act out of character)*
der Schatten, -	shadow
springen*	to spring, jump
die Höflichkeit, -en	courtesy, politeness
Höflichkeit ist gut und schön, aber weiter kommt man ohne sie.	Politeness is all well and good, but one gets further without it.
weiterkommen*	to come/go further

A 3

die Satzeinleitung, -en	lead-in/opening to a sentence
zurückgeben* (du gibst zurück, er gibt zurück)	to give back
Wir haben uns neulich mißverstanden.	We had a misunderstanding a few days ago.
(sich) **mißverstehen*** (du mißverstehst mich)	to misunderstand, to have a misunderstanding
Der Ton macht die Musik.	It's not what you say but the way that you say it.
der Ton ⁻e	tone; sound
bitten*	to ask

A 4

der Infinitivsatz, ⁻e	infinitive sentence
persönlich	personal
unpersönlich	impersonal
ein Mißverständnis klären	to clear up a misunderstanding
klären	to clear up, clarify

A 5

sich erinnern an	to remember
Frau L fällt es schwer, . . .	Mrs L finds it difficult . . .
schwerfallen* *(unpersönlich:* es fällt mir schwer)	to find it difficult to . . .

A 6

Europa	Europe
der Erdteil, -e	continent
der Engländer, - (in f)	Englishman/-woman
Asien	Asia
Nordamerika	North America
Südamerika	South America
Afrika	Africa

132

A 7 die Konvention, -en	convention
das Schweinefleisch	pork
verboten sein	to be forbidden
B 1 lügen*	to lie, to tell lies
ehrlich	honest
jedesmal	always, every time
bedauernswert	unfortunate, pitiable
Ich habe ja selbst schuld.	It is my own fault.
schuld haben*	to be guilty
loben	to praise
extra für Sie	especially for you
extra	extra, special
die Andeutung, -en	hint, indication
die Magenschmerzen	stomach-ache
der Magen, -	stomach
Gott sei Dank!	Thank God!
der Gott, ⁻er	God
der Lieblingskuchen, -	favourite cake
der Spruch, ⁻e	saying, aphorism; *in the Bible:* Proverbs

Eure Rede aber sei ja, ja, nein, nein. Was darüber ist, das ist von Übel.	Let your word be 'Yes' when you mean 'Yes', and 'No' when you mean 'No'; anything more than that comes from the evil one.
Matthäus 5, 37	Matthew, Chapter, 5, Verse 37

die Rede, -n	word, speech, utterance
das Übel, -	evil
die Bibel, -n	The Bible
das Neue Testament	The New Testament

Da lob ich mir die Höflichkeit, Das zierliche Betrügen. Du weißt Bescheid, ich weiß Bescheid: Und allen macht's Vergnügen.	That I praise politeness, The elegant deception, You know, I know: And it all makes good fun.

betrügen*	to deceive

14

Bescheid wissen*   to know

> **Bescheid wissen – jemandem Bescheid sagen**
> Alle wußten Bescheid, nur ich nicht!
> Everybody knew except me!
>
> Sag mir bitte Bescheid, wann du kommst.
> Please tell me when you are coming.

	die Harmonie, -n	harmony
	das Geschenk, -e	present, gift
B 3	**die Wahrheit, -en**	truth
	aussprechen* (du sprichst aus, er spricht aus)	to express, declare, say
	Ich Kamel!	What a blockhead I am!
	das Kamel, -e	camel
	Die dumme Kuh!	The silly cow!
	die Kuh, ̈e	cow
	in Wirklichkeit	in reality
	die Wirklichkeit, -en	reality
	Ich Esel!	What a silly ass I am!
	der Esel, -	ass, donkey
	Ich armer Hund!	What a poor devil I am!
	So ein schlauer Fuchs!	Such a sly fox!
	schlau	sly, cunning
	der Fuchs, ̈e	fox
	geduldig wie ein Lamm sein	to be as patient as a lamb
	geduldig	patient
	das Lamm, ̈er	lamb
	ein Elefant im Porzellanladen sein	to be a bull (!) in a china shop
	der Elefant, -en	elephant
	das Porzellan	porcelain, china
	der Laden, ̈	shop
B 4	die Eigenschaft, -en	quality, characteristic
B 5	**schimpfen** (= beschimpfen)	*here:* to insult, scold, abuse
	Pfui!	Shame on you!
	problematisch	problematic
	Armes Schwein!	Poor devil!
	das Schwein, -e	pig, swine
	der Schmutz	filth, dirt
	die Schweinerei, -en	mess; scandal
	überlegen	to consider, think about

> **Das Kamel**
>
> | | |
> |---|---|
> | Bedauernswert ist das Kamel! | The camel is a pitiful creature! |
> | – Das Tier muß es ertragen, | The animal must put up with the fact |
> | daß seine Freunde, geht was fehl, | That whatever goes amiss, his friends |
> | „Du Mensch" verächtlich sagen. | Say scornfully, "What a human being!" |

B 6	das Rollenspiel, -e	role-play
B 7	**schenken**	to give as a present
	das Kuchenrezept, -e	cake recipe
	unfreundlich	unfriendly
	unehrlich	dishonest, unreliable
B 8	**der Schalter, -**	counter *(in a bank, etc.)*
B 9	**die Situation, -en**	situation
C 1	der Zoobesucher, - (in f)	visitor to a zoo
	Das ist ja ein wunderschönes Tier!	That's a very beautiful animal.
	wunderschön	very beautiful, lovely
	das Schaf, -e	sheep
	das Mondschaf, -e	moon-sheep *(Reference to a nonsense poem by Christian Morgenstern.)*
	fressen*(du frißt, er frißt)	to eat *(used of animals)*
	die Partikel, -n	particle
	staunen	to be astonished
	drohen	to threaten
	die Übereinstimmung, -en	agreement, conformity
C 2	der Spaßmacher, - (in f)	wag, joker
	Franz	*a male first name*
	einmal, zweimal, x-mal	once, twice, x-times
	informell	informal
C 3	Julia	Juliet
	Eigentlich sollte ich so heißen, aber . . .	Actually that's what I should be called, but . . .
	Romeo	Romeo *(The dialogue plays with the names of the main characters in Shakespeare's drama: Romeo and Juliet.)*

14

C 4	**lieben**	to love
	Tja, . . .	*a sound indicating that something is being considered*
	der Cartoon, -s	cartoon
	frauenfeindlich	anti-women
	die Einschränkung, -en	restriction, limitation
	die Modifizierung, -en	modification
	die Entscheidung, -en	decision
	die Absicht, -en	intention
C 5	das Lehrwerk, - e	textbook
	die Aufforderung, -en	request
	versuchen	to try
	der Gesprächspartner, - (in f)	partner, person taking part in a discussion
	zurückkommen* (ich komme zurück)	to come back
C 6	Uschi	*the short form of the female first name* Ursula
	Willy	*the short form of the male first name* Wilhelm
	die Weltreise, -n	world tour
	Helmut	*a male first name*
	Singapur	Singapore
C 7	die Partikeljagd, -en	the hunt for particles
D 1	der Ehepartner, - (in f)	marriage partner *(i.e. husband or wife)*
	Jahrgang 1936	born in 1936
	der Jahrgang, ⁻e	age group, year's class, *etc*
	Aachen	Aachen
	die Heiratsanzeige, -n	marriage announcement; *here: the announcement of the wish to find a partner*
	das Dorf, ⁻er	village
	eine Anzeige aufgeben	to put an advertisement in *(a newspaper)*
	die Anzeige, -n	notice, announcement
	aufgeben* (du gibst auf, er gibt auf)	to hand in, deliver
	die Ehe, -n	the marriage
	Unsere Ehe hält schon über 25 Jahre.	Our marriage has already lasted over 25 years.
	halten* *(i. d. Bed. nur 3. Person Sg. und Pl.)*	to last, hold

die Silberhochzeit, -en	silver wedding (anniversary)
Zuschriften unter . . .	letters/communication to . . .
der Musiklehrer, - (in f)	music teacher
das Elternhaus, ¨-er	parents' house
konservativ	conservative
der Heiratsvermittler, - (in f)	marriage broker
engagieren	to engage
Das erinnert mich ein bißchen an unsere Tradition.	That reminds me a little of our tradition.
jemanden an etwas erinnern	to remind someone of something

---

jemanden an etwas/jemanden erinnern
to remind someone of something/someone

Sie erinnerte ihn sehr an seine erste Liebe.
She reminded him very much of his first love.

sich an etwas/jemanden erinnern
to remember something/someone

Er konnte sich nicht an seine erste Liebe erinnern.
He couldn't remember his first love.

---

die Tradition, -en	tradition
der Diplomchemiker, - (in f)	person with a diploma in chemistry
Marokko	Morocco
der Posten, -	post, position, job
ewig	forever
verwandt sein	to be related
entfernt verwandt sein	to be distantly related
aussuchen (ich suche aus)	to look for, to seek out
sich trennen von + *Dat.*	to separate oneself from, to leave
Blaubeuren	*a town near Ulm (See map inside back cover of textbook.)*
Wir haben uns sofort hoffnungslos ineinander verliebt.	We immediately fell hopelessly in love.
hoffnungslos	hopeless(ly)
sich ineinander verlieben	to fall in love with one another
ohne Trauschein zusammenleben	to live together without getting married
der Trauschein, -e	marriage certificate
zusammenleben (wir leben zusammen)	to live together

14

	das Standesamt, ⸚er	Registry Office
	Ulm	Ulm *(See map inside back cover of textbook.)*
	staatlich	state, belonging to the state
	die Behörde, -n	government department, office
	die Geburt, -en	birth
	die Heirat, -en	marriage
D 3	**als** *(Subjunktor)*	when *(as a connector)*
	die Gegenwart	present
	die Zukunft	future
D 4	die Liebesgeschichte, -n	love story
D 5	**wegsehen*** (du siehst weg, er sieht weg)	to look away
	sitzenbleiben* (ich bleibe sitzen)	to remain seated
D 6	der Schlager, -	popular song
D 7	die Parkbank, ⸚e	park bench
	die Bank, ⸚e	*here:* seat, bench
E	das Sprichwort, ⸚er	proverb, saying
	Liebe macht blind.	Love is blind.
	ungewiß	uncertain
	der Mund, ⸚er	mouth
	ausrechnen (ich rechne aus)	to calculate
	Schreiben Sie das Gedicht bitte um!	Please rewrite the poem.
	umschreiben*	to rewrite
	das Liebesgedicht, -e	love poem
	die Assoziation, -en	association
♪ 4	die Grundtendenz, -en	basic tendency
	die Tendenz, -en	tendency

A 1 der Halb‗drachen, - — half-dragon *(Metaphor for a creature that consists of two different halves.)*

das Nilpferd, -e — hippopotamus
der Krokodil‗schwanz, ⸚e — crocodile tail
einsam — solitary, lonely
der Vulkan, -e — volcano
Man sah es mir an. — People could tell by looking at me.

jemandem etwas an‗sehen* — to see something about someone
In einer einheitlichen Welt fällt das auf. — In a uniform world that attracts attention.
einheitlich — uniform, standardized
auf‗fallen* (du fällst auf, er fällt auf) — to attract attention, be noticable
nach‗rufen* (ich rufe nach) — to call out after
entdecken — to discover
der Mangel, ⸚ — deficiency, lack
der Reichtum, ⸚er — riches, abundance
Ich bin arm und reich zugleich. — I am poor and rich at the same time.
zugleich — at the same time
Ich bin weder noch, ich bin beides. — I am neither, I am both.
auf‗wachsen* (du wächst auf, er wächst auf) — to grow up
die Volks‗republik, -en — People's Republic

A 2 Koestler, Arthur (1905–1982) — *writer*
Budapest — Budapest
der Ungar, -n (in f) — Hungarian (man/woman)
die Kindheit, -en — childhood
Ungarn — Hungary
der Korrespondent, -en (in f) — correspondent
der Zeitungs‗verlag, -e — newspaper publishing house
der Emigrant, -en (in f) — emigrant
die Emigration — emigration
von Land zu Land wechseln — to switch/change from country to country

wechseln — to change
fleißig — diligent
Ungarisch — Hungarian
fließend — fluent
eine Sprache fließend sprechen — to speak a language fluently
das Lebens‗jahr, -e — year of (one's) life
einen starken Einfluß ausüben — to exercise a strong influence

der Einfluß, Einflüsse	influence
ausüben	to exercise, exert
kindlich	childlike
schriftstellerische Versuche	attempts at writing, literary attempts
schriftstellerisch	to do with writing, literary
der Versuch, -e	attempt
Wir zogen nach Wien.	We moved to Vienna.
ziehen*	to move

---

ziehen

Er zieht seine Jacke aus.
He is taking his jacket off.

Familie Koestler zog nach Wien.
The Koestler family moved to Vienna.

Ich bin viel zu warm angezogen.
I'm much too warmly dressed.

Herr Tossu zieht Herrn Klinger durch den Kakao.
Mr Tossu makes Mr Klinger look a little bit ridiculous.

---

eine Schule besuchen	to go to a school, to attend a school
besuchen	to visit; *here:* attend, go to
allmählich	gradual(ly), by degrees
reimen	to rhyme
die Erzählung, -en	story
von jetzt an	from now *(ie. then)* onwards
von . . . an	from . . . onwards
der Übergang, ⸚e	transition
„Sonnenfinsternis"	*This novel by Koestler is called* "Darkness at Noon" *in English.*
eine Art Gettoexistenz	a form of ghetto existence
die Existenz, -en	existence
das Getto, -s	ghetto
der Flüchtling, -e	refugee
träumen	to dream
vielsprachig	multi-lingual
das Kauderwelsch	mishmash; gibberish
A 3 **der Abschnitt, -e**	section; paragraph
A 4 die eckige Klammer	square brackets
eckig	with corners, square
die Klammer, -n	bracket

A 6 die Wieder‿aufnahme, -n	resumption
etwas wieder auf‿nehmen* (du nimmst auf, er nimmt auf)	to resume something
verkürzt	shortened, abridged
A 7 die Sprach‿biographie, -n	language biography
Kairo	Cairo
privat	private
Alle Kinder sprachen Spanisch, wenn sie unter sich waren.	All the children spoke Spanish when they were among themselves.
Genf	Geneva
der Übersetzer, - (in f)	translator
A 8 **die Überschrift, -en**	title, heading
Amor	*Portuguese for 'love'*
aus‿wandern (ich wandere aus)	to migrate
der Abgrund, ⁻e	abyss
zurück‿kehren (ich kehre zurück)	to return
der Auswanderer, - (Auswanderin f)	emigrant
B 1 gastlich	hospitable
gesamt	whole, entire
die Menschheit	human race, humanity
nicht nur . . ., sondern auch . . .	not only . . . but also . . .
das Steak, -s	steak
die Sauce, -n	sauce
die Pflaume, -n	plum
die Kirsche, -n	cherry
Lateinisch	Latin
die Dattel, -n	date *(fruit)*
Skythisch	Scythian
der Quark	curd cheese
Polnisch	Polish
das Rebhuhn, ⁻er	partridge
holländisch	Dutch
der Matjes, -	white herring
= der Matjeshering, -e	
der Joghurt	joghurt
das Gulasch	goulash
die Kongo‿sprache, -n	the Congolese language
der Kongo	Congo
die Kaper, -n	caper
Persisch	Persian
die Mandel, -n	almond
Syrisch	Syrian

der Zimt	cinnamon
Malayisch	Malayan, Malaysian
die Mayasprache	the language of the Maya
indianisch	Indian
der Grog, -s	grog
der Kognak, -s	cognac
der Sekt	champagne or sparkling wine
der Arrak	arrack or arak *(a spirit distilled from grain)*
das Känguruh, -s	kangaroo
Australisch	Australian
Rußland	Russia
der Hering, -e	herring
B 2 der Brunnen, -	well, fountain
Das Wort wird umgetrieben.	The word will be driven around.
umtreiben*	to rotate, spin, drive around
eine Farbe annehmen	to take on a colour
annehmen* (du nimmst an, er nimmt an)	to take or to receive
heimisch	home-bred, native, indigenous
Grimm, Jacob (1785–1863)	*German language scholar; with his brother Wilhelm he published the* Kinder- und Hausmärchen, *known in English as 'Grimms' Fairy Tales', and the 'German Dictionary' –* Deutsches Wörterbuch.
B 3 der Sprachaustausch	language exchange
die Hängematte, -n	hammock
Der Schein trügt.	Appearances are deceptive.
der Schein	look, appearance
trügen*	to deceive, to be misleading
stammen aus + *Dat.*	to come/originate from
Haiti	Haiti
Kolumbus, Christoph (1451–1506)	*Sea-farer from Genoa, Italy, who in 1492 sailed under the patronage of Ferdinand and Isabella of Spain to look for the New World.*
die Matte, -n	mat
B 4 der Vordere Orient	the Near East
der Römer, - (in f)	Roman
vorderasiatisch	Near Eastern

C 1	die Verbstellung, -en	position of the verb
	die Stellung, -en	position
	Das hängt von vielen Faktoren ab.	That is dependent on many factors.
	der Faktor, -en	factor
	abhängen* von + *Dat.*	to be dependent on
	das Mittelfeld, -er	middle field
	die Linkstendenz, -en	left tendency
	die Rechtstendenz, -en	right tendency
C 2	die Vorinformation, -en	preliminary information
	enthalten* *(i. d. Bed. nur 3. Person Sg. und Pl.: er enthält)*	to contain, comprise
	die Rose, -n	rose
	tendieren	to tend, to be inclined
C 5	unbetontes Personalpronomen	unstressed personal pronoun
	die Grundfolge, -n	basic order
	das Deutschlehrbuch, ̈-er	German textbook
D 1	**die Schrift, -en**	(type of) writing
	Wie befindet sich Ihre werte Gemahlin?	How is your esteemed wife?
	sich befinden*	to be, to find yourself *(condition)*
	der Gemahl, die Gemahlin	husband, wife; *old terms equivalent to 'consort' or 'spouse'*
	Empfehlen Sie mich ergebenst.	Give my most humble respects to . . .
D 2	die Jugendsprache, -en	the language of youth
	Mensch, . . .	Hey, . . .
	Irre, was?	That's crazy, don't you think?
	bloß (= nur)	only
	der Typ, -en (= der Mann)	type *(meaning a person)*
	die Alte, -n (= die Frau)	old lady
	Echt stark!	Really strong stuff!
	der/die Jugendliche, -n	young people, youth
	der/die Erwachsene, -n	adult
	Was soll da erst ein Ausländer sagen, der gerade anfängt, Deutsch zu lernen.	What is a foreigner who has just started to learn German supposed to say.

---

gerade

Sie hat sich gerade von ihrem Mann getrennt.
She has just left her husband.

Er streckte seinen Arm und sagte: „Das ist gerade.".
He stretched out his arm and said: "That is straight."

Moderne Möbel haben gerade Formen und klare Linien.
Modern furniture has straightforward forms and clear lines.

Warum gefällt dir gerade dieses Buch?
Why do you like this book in particular?

---

die Höflichkeitsformel, -n	polite phrase
veraltet	old, aged
Was sagen Sie stattdessen?	What do you say instead?
Wir verzichten lieber darauf.	We prefer to do without them.
verzichten auf + *Akk.*	to do without, dispense with
D 4 Gib mal den Zucker rüber, Kleine.	Pass the sugar over, Shorty.
rübergeben = herübergeben	to pass over/across
Würden Sie mir den Zucker reichen?	Would you please pass me the sugar?
reichen	to reach; *here:* to pass over/on to someone
die Empfangsdame, -n	(lady) receptionist
der Empfang, ̈e	reception
Gestatten Sie?	Have I your permission? May I?
gestatten	to permit, allow
der Tanz, ̈e	dance
D 5 Co. = Compagnie	Company
Der Spiegel	The Mirror *(News magazine which appears once a week.)*
etwas verlernen	to forget something *(learned earlier)*
neutrales Deutsch	neutral German
jemanden ansprechen* (du sprichst an, er spricht an)	to address someone
E 1 perfekt	perfect
Kolumbien	Colombia *(South America)*
das Argument, -e	argument
die Verständlichkeit	intelligibility, being understood
♪ **1** so weit wie möglich	as far as possible
♪ **2** in Klammern setzen	put in brackets